G.O.A.T.

MAKING THE CASE FOR THE GREATEST OF ALL TIME

TOM
BRADY

BY BOB GURNETT

STERLING CHILDREN'S BOOKS
New York

STERLING CHILDREN'S BOOKS
New York

An Imprint of Sterling Publishing Co., Inc.
1166 Avenue of the Americas
New York, NY 10036

33614082297895

ISBN 978-1-4549-3099-0

Distributed in Canada by Sterling Publishing Co., Inc.
c/o Canadian Manda Group, 664 Annette Street
Toronto, Ontario M6S 2C8, Canada
Distributed in the United Kingdom by GMC Distribution Services
Castle Place, 166 High Street, Lewes, East Sussex BN7 1XU, England
Distributed in Australia by NewSouth Books
University of New South Wales, Sydney, NSW 2052, Australia

For information about custom editions, special sales, and premium
and corporate purchases, please contact Sterling Special Sales at
800-805-5489 or specialsales@sterlingpublishing.com.

Manufactured in China

Lot #:
2 4 6 8 10 9 7 5 3 1
05/20

sterlingpublishing.com

Cover and interior design by Heather Kelly

Image credits are on page 128

CONTENTS

WHAT IS A
G.O.A.T?

Most people do not want to be compared to a barnyard animal, but a G.O.A.T. is different. These G.O.A.T.s aren't found in petting zoos, but you can see them on the gridiron, the hardwood, the ice, and the diamond. G.O.A.T. is an acronym that stands for Greatest of All Time. It takes lifelong dedication, non-stop hard work, and undeniable talent just to become a professional athlete. But to become the greatest of all time, well, that's nearly impossible. There are a handful of athletes who are widely thought to be the G.O.A.T. of their sport. Swimmer Michael Phelps moves like a fish in water, but he is also the G.O.A.T. with 23 Olympic gold medals, the most of all time. Tennis player Serena Williams is the G.O.A.T. with 23 Grand Slam titles in the Open Era, more than any woman *or* man.

But for some sports, a G.O.A.T. is not as easy to identify and fans may disagree about who is the greatest of all time. If you asked five baseball fans who the greatest baseball player of all time is, you might get five or more different answers—say, Babe Ruth, Willie Mays, Barry

Bonds, Cy Young, Lou Gehrig, or maybe rising young superstar Mike Trout. The G.O.A.T. may change, depending on who is asked, and what that person's reasons, or criteria, are. Babe Ruth won seven World Series, had a .342 lifetime batting average, and is still in third place all time for home runs, even though he retired over 80 years ago, in 1935. Willie Mays did not have the same prowess at the plate as Ruth, but he is still considered the best defensive player in history. Different players, different achievements, but both are still the greatest at what they did. Fans will disagree as to who the true G.O.A.T. is, but to even be considered for this distinction, a player must be one of the best to ever live.

Football has its own G.O.A.T. debate. Ask 20 people and you may get 20 different answers on who is the greatest football player of all time. Is it Peyton Manning? He holds almost every regular-season passing record. Is it Jerry Rice? He has more all-purpose yards than any player ever. Maybe it is Lawrence Taylor, the fierce defensive back who once recorded over 20 sacks in a season. If you ask this question, a lot of people will say the G.O.A.T. isn't in the Hall of Fame because he is still playing at a very high level, even in his early 40s. New England quarterback Tom Brady certainly has a claim to the mantle of G.O.A.T. Let's review the evidence, for and against, and see if you agree!

1

LITTLE TOMMY

The Brady household in San Mateo, California, was known as a house of athletes, and those athletes were named Maureen, Nancy, and Julie. Tom Brady, future six-time Super Bowl champion? He was just "Little Tommy."

Tom Brady is the youngest of four kids. His three older sisters were all star athletes. His oldest sister, Maureen, was on the US Junior Olympics softball team. Nancy and Julie were soccer and softball standouts. Tommy was their little brother, who followed them to all their games. He was the boy who loved to go fishing with his uncles in Minnesota. When Tom once wrote a school paper that, someday, he wanted to be a household name, everyone thought it was funny. No one knew how serious he was. No one had any idea that not too many years later people would call him the G.O.A.T.

A teenage Tom Brady. Tom started playing organized football at the age of 14.

Thomas Edward Patrick Brady Jr. was born in 1977. The youngest of four, and the only boy, he was named after his dad. Little Tommy loved football, especially his San Francisco 49ers. His family had season tickets, and, every Sunday, Tommy and his dad would watch their favorite football player, Joe Montana, on the **gridiron**. In the 1980s, a lot of people thought Joe Montana was the G.O.A.T. Montana threw precise passes all over the field. His long bombs to streaking receivers always landed right where they needed to. Short, high-speed throws hit a crossing **tight end** in traffic, where no one else had a chance to get to it. More important than his accuracy, Joe Montana refused to lose. He went to the Super Bowl four times and never lost. Little Tommy wanted to be just like him one day.

It may come as a surprise, but Tom Brady didn't play organized football until he was 14 years old. He was smaller and slower than a lot of the other boys at Junipero Serra High School in San Mateo. That didn't stop him from trying out to be the **quarterback** in his freshman year, and making the junior varsity team. But Tom didn't get a chance to play. His JV team went 0–8 and never scored a touchdown. No one thought Tom had much of a future in football. Everyone just assumed that he would keep playing baseball. He was, after all, a superstar left-handed catcher, and he hit for power, at a school known for producing extraordinary Major League Baseball players, like Barry Bonds. An MLB scout even thought Tom could have been one of the greatest MLB catchers of all time. It seemed that football was just for fun and baseball was his calling. But Little Tommy didn't see it that way. He was anxious to take his football talent to the next level.

In Tom's sophomore year, the starting quarterback quit the team. The team was dismal, so no one else wanted to be its quarterback, either. Tom became the starting quarterback by default. Suddenly, the kid everyone knew as Maureen Brady's little brother was in the spotlight. He was the starter for the rest of his high school career. His teams were not outstanding, but they did improve from the dreadful 0–8 record Tom's freshman year. His junior and senior years, their records were 6–4 and 5–5.

Tom Brady was hardly the most athletic player. He wasn't the biggest player. But he was the best player on the team because he worked the hardest. He knew his coaches thought he was too slow, so he spent hours honing his fitness routine to get better. His high school coach, Tom McKenzie, used a technique during practice called the Five-Dot Drill. It helped kids with foot speed. The drill consisted of moving around five dots on the ground as fast as the players could. Tom wanted so badly to improve his speed that he asked his coach for the diagram of the drill. He then spray-painted the five dots on his back patio at home. His sisters said he would stay up every night doing the drill until he had to go inside. This is just one example of the many ways Tom was committed to becoming a better football player.

Tom (top row, center) in his senior year with his high school team.

Not only was Tom determined to make himself a better player, but he wanted to make everyone on his team better players. The quarterback of a football team isn't just another player. He is the signal-caller and the team leader. Tom took that responsibility very seriously. John Kirby, one of Tom Brady's top receivers in high school, praised Tom's leadership. Kirby said Tom spent a lot of time keeping the team together and building up everyone's self-esteem. Tom believed in each player and in the team as a whole. That mind-set made everyone around him better. His leadership was one of the qualities that made him stand out from other players. Leadership is just one of the **intangibles**, or skills that can't be measured by statistics or on tape, that coaches loved about him.

Tom's work ethic is something that never changed from high school. He was constantly looking for ways to bring his game to the next level. If someone noticed a flaw in his game, he would work tirelessly to fix it. Coach McKenzie said he coached a lot of better athletes in his career but he never coached a better football player. McKenzie wasn't the only one to spot Tom's potential. College scouts had noticed, too. Football coaches at major colleges, like the University of Southern California, the University of California at Berkeley, and the University of Michigan, had all seen tapes of Tom, sent to them by his dad, Tom Sr. He put together highlight tapes demonstrating Tom's arm strength and accuracy. The tapes included long bombs, short passes, and everything in between. Scouts at USC and Michigan were so impressed that both made offers for him to come play as a **Division I** quarterback!

COLLEGE FOOTBALL RECRUITING

College football is divided into divisions. Division 1 is the highest division, but even that has a highest group, called the Football Bowl Subdivision (FBS). The college football games broadcast on TV on fall Saturdays usually showcase Division 1 FBS teams. That is the highest and most competitive college football subdivision and features the biggest and best football schools in the country.

These top schools work hard to recruit the best athletes in the country. Coaches and staff members travel the country to scout for gifted players to recruit for their team. From there, they will set up meetings to try to convince players that their school is the best school for them. The school will usually offer them full scholarships, completely paying for their schooling. The best athletes get offers from multiple schools and then have to decide which program and school are their best fit. If a player isn't recruited, it doesn't mean he can't play football! A walk-on is an athlete who didn't receive a scholarship but made the team anyway!

The recruiting process was hard for Tom. He desperately wanted to play for a Division I school. He also felt pressure because he was drafted by a Major League Baseball team, the Montreal Expos, in 1995. Tom had made it clear that football was his passion, so no one expected him to take the Expos' offer, no matter how tempting. His dad reasoned that there was a good chance he would not become a professional football player, so he'd better get a degree from a good school. It wasn't that his dad didn't believe in Tom. He just wanted to make sure that if Tom didn't become a successful football player, he could still be proud of his education. So Tom decided to take his talents to Michigan. He knew the leap from high school would be big, but he had no idea how big it would be until he stepped onto the field in front of 100,000 cheering fans.

2

JUST ANOTHER GUY

From the moment Tom Brady got to the University of Michigan in 1996, he was just another guy. The head coach and recruiter who had convinced Tom to come to Michigan were no longer with the university. Tom had no one in his corner when he walked into the locker room for the first time. Brady didn't have anyone rooting against him. He just didn't have anyone rooting for him. Tom spent his first season as a **red shirt**, meaning that he did not play in games but still practiced with the team. He spent that year working to make himself better, both physically and mentally. He made use of the team's sports psychologist to help him adjust to college life and learn to handle the new stress of competing for the starting quarterback job.

The 6-foot-4 Brady started his post–red shirt career as the backup for quarterback Brian Griese (who would later play in the NFL). Tom was never going to take the reins from such an accomplished quarterback. So he used that time to learn from the coaches and to learn from Brian. It is easy to look back and second-guess what the new Michigan coach, Lloyd Carr, was thinking playing Brian Griese over Tom Brady, but Brady's coach had no idea how much he'd grown as a quarterback. Even then, he recognized Brady's mental toughness. Coach Carr couldn't think of a player who could have handled the challenges he faced as a backup quarterback better.

This didn't mean that Tom didn't have his doubts. He even considered transferring to another school where he

Tom Brady would eventually become starting quarterback for the University of Michigan.

could get playing time. But his dad had taught him to never run from his problems and instead face them head-on. So he went into Coach Carr's office and told him he was going to stay at Michigan and prove to Carr that he was a great quarterback.

And that's what Tom set out to do. He came to practice every day to show everyone that he was a great quarterback. More than that, Tom set out to prove to them that he was a great leader. Jay Feely, the Michigan kicker, said his leadership was obvious to everyone. Just like Tom's high school teammates, Feely said Tom brought everyone together. Even as a third-string quarterback, Tom encouraged and supported his teammates.

At the start of his junior year, he thought his time had finally come. The Michigan Wolverines had won the national championship the year before and starting QB Brian Griese went off to the Denver Broncos in the NFL. Tom thought he was the obvious choice. Instead, Michigan recruited a hometown hero, a highly touted prospect named Drew Henson. Henson went to high school less than an hour outside of Ann Arbor, where the University of Michigan is located. He was one of the top prospects in all of football. Right before the start of the season, Coach Carr told the press that Drew Henson was his pick for the starting QB position. This was unwelcome news for Tom: there would be a competition for the starting quarterback spot.

Fans and local sports reporters were excited about Henson. He had been featured in *Sports Illustrated*. Like Tom, Henson had been drafted by a Major League Baseball team (in his case, by the New York Yankees), but decided to play football instead. Tom realized that he did not have the job locked up. So he used the competition as a source of motivation. Tom knew that competing against the best could only make him better. He gave his all at practice every day. He stayed up late watching film and was up every morning at six o'clock to work out. He showed his coaches that he was ready and eager to get the start. Even though Tom was picked to start the first game of the season, he knew that he didn't have the job locked up. He would have to be the best quarterback he could be.

On September 5, 1998, Tom stepped onto the turf for his first game as the Michigan Wolverines' starting quarterback. They were playing against Notre Dame, and he was determined to prove himself, Tom hit six of seven passes on the opening **drive**. He went 57 yards, throwing quick short passes and nailing his receivers in stride. Tom played spectacularly, but the offense stalled out. They settled for a field goal and were up by three. Notre Dame answered with a field goal of their own. The next two Wolverine possessions, Tom drove his team within field-goal range again. The starting kicker, Kraig Baker, missed both kicks, and they were still tied 3–3. The next drive, Tom threw a long pass, the kind he put in his recruitment video: 42 yards to Marcus Knight! It was the longest he had ever thrown in college. The team was again in field-goal range. After missing two field goals in a row, Carr put in Jay Feely, Baker's backup. Tom took notice—anyone, not just a quarterback, could lose his spot at any moment. Jay hit the field goal and would be the starting kicker for the rest of the season. Kraig was replaced, just like that.

The next drive, Tom took his team 72 yards on 12 plays. The offense drove all the way to the 1-yard line. Tom was so close to the end zone that he could spit in it. After so many missed opportunities, Tom knew he had to do it himself. He called for the snap and his whole offensive line shoved and moved forward against the defense. This mighty push opened up just enough room. From the 1-yard line, with 23 seconds left in the half, Tom plunged into the end zone behind his offensive line. A QB sneak. The slow runner from San Mateo with a great arm had his first college football touchdown: a 1-yard **rush**, and Michigan took a 13–6 lead at halftime.

Tom didn't have too much time to celebrate. The Wolverines could not hold onto the ball on their next two possessions after the intermission. After back-to-back fumbles by his fullback and kick receiver, the Wolverines were way down. Notre Dame had scored 17 unanswered points in the third quarter, for a 23–13 lead. The Wolverines were too far down to come back, so Coach Carr pulled Tom from the game late in the fourth quarter, with Notre Dame leading 36–13. He put in Drew Henson. Henson led an 80-yard touchdown drive, capping it off with an 8-yard touchdown pass just before the game ended in a 36–20 Michigan loss.

Despite the loss, the newspapers reported on how great Drew Henson had been. Tom Brady went 23 for 26, only missing on three passes, and scored a rushing touchdown, but the story of the day was the freshman Henson. Even with amazing play, Tom was losing ground to Henson in the quarterback competition.

Tom's next game was even worse. Syracuse dismantled the Michigan defense. At one point, Tom was hit hard. He was taken out of the game for a few series and, once again, Drew Hensen took over the team. The record-setting hometown crowd cheered loudly. A few series of possessions later, Tom was put back into the game. The crowd booed him. Tom felt like a visiting quarterback right at home in Ann Arbor. In front of 100,000 people, Tom Brady was all alone. Michigan lost the game 28–38.

The quarterback controversy was the lead story in every paper in Ann Arbor and much of the country after that game. Tom had already been benched twice. Would he be like the kicker, Kraig Baker, and be benched for good? How could he lead his team if he kept getting benched? After all, his team had voted him as one of their three captains. They all looked to him for guidance. If he was sharing time with a rookie, would it undermine his leadership? Carr eventually saw this and named Brady the sole starter for the rest of the season. It was Tom's time to lead the team. So he did.

After the announcement, Tom led the team to eight straight wins, including wins against the #9- and #8-ranked teams in the country. Tom told reporters that he was not focused on beating out Drew, but instead was determined to be the best football player he could be. And he was. Tom ended the season completing 62 percent of his passes for 2,427 yards and throwing for 14 touchdowns. No matter what the home crowd wanted, that team was Brady's team. He won and kept on winning. The team finished 10–3. They won a share of the Big 10 title and went on to win the Citrus Bowl

against Arkansas. Still, Tom knew deep down that that did not mean the quarterback job was his. He had to fight for the job again the next season. He just didn't know how hard he'd have to fight.

Tom Brady with fellow University of Michigan quarterbacks Drew Henson (far left) and Jason Kapsner (left).

BOWL GAMES

The very first bowl game was played in 1902 as part of the Tournament of Rose Festival in Pasadena, California. The game itself was nothing special: a 49–0 rout of Stanford by Michigan. The festival organizers did not bring football back until 1916 and the game got so popular that it was moved to the newly constructed Rose Bowl Stadium. The New Year's Day game was called a "bowl game" because of its location. The name stuck.

Now, a bowl game refers to a number of postseason college football games. The games are big postseason matchups that are widely watched. Initially created to be fun exhibition games, bowl games have grown into huge spectacles and massive moneymakers. A handful of those bowl games make up the National Collegiate Athletic Association (NCAA) playoffs to decide the national champion.

However, when Tom was playing for Michigan, there was no playoff. Instead, at the end of the season, a combination of polling and computer rankings picked the top two teams for just one game, the Bowl Championship Series (BCS) National Championship game.

At the start of the 1999 season, Carr announced that Tom and Henson would take turns playing quarterback. Tom and Henson would play in alternating quarters. At halftime in every game, Carr would decide who played the second half. Carr later recalled how well Tom handled that decision. As always, Tom displayed maturity and grace. When the season started, Drew Henson was confident that he would win the starting job from Brady. He told the press that he respected Tom, but it was a new year and a new season. The pressure to be the best had never been so great for Tom.

In this new, strange system, Tom was picked to play the second half both times. Each time, Tom was booed by the Ann Arbor fans. He still won both games. Then in game 3 against Syracuse, Drew Henson was picked to lead the team in the second half. Tom waited on the sideline and watched his rival lead Michigan to a big win. Coach Carr remembers that game as the time he witnessed the most amazing example of leadership he ever saw in athletics. Except he wasn't talking about Henson. He was talking about Tom Brady, who after the game rallied the team around Henson and the great win. The team looked to Tom, their captain, for leadership. Tom hated not being on the field, but knew it was for the good of the team.

Henson would only get the second-half nod one more time. In a game against Michigan State, Henson blew a lead and Tom returned to the game to clean up the mess. He almost salvaged it, but the damage had been done. The Wolverines lost 31–34 and Carr stopped using the rotation system. It was clear that Tom was the best quarterback they had. The team was his. Some people were surprised by this move, but not any of the players on the Wolverines. As far as they were concerned, the quarterback spot always belonged to their captain, Tom Brady.

The Wolverines would only lose one more time that season. Michigan ended the regular season with four straight wins before facing the University of Alabama's Crimson Tide in the Orange Bowl. Early on, the Wolverines fell behind 14–0. Tom was getting knocked around by the fierce Alabama defense, but he kept getting back up. He put together back-to-back drives to bring the game to a 14–14 tie. The second touchdown was on a 3rd and 8 play. Tom was being blitzed by the Alabama linebackers. Even though they were closing in, Tom stood tall in the **pocket** and threw a 57-yard touchdown pass. Michigan was right back in the game.

At the end of regulation play, the score was tied at 28. They were going into overtime for the first time in Michigan football history. On the very first play of overtime, Tom decided to show the Michigan fans one last time why he had won the quarterback spot. The ball was snapped. Tom faked the run handoff, then rolled right with the ball. Alabama blitzed again. Three huge Alabama defenders closed in on him. Far behind the defenders, he saw his tight end, Shawn Thompson, get a few inches of separation from his defender. Tom threw the pass above the defenders. It landed directly in the outstretched hands of his tight end. Thompson ran untouched into the end zone for the touchdown. This was the first play of overtime in the biggest game of Tom's career, and he threw a perfect pass to take the lead for good. Tom watched anxiously from the sidelines as Alabama scored a touchdown but missed their extra point. The game was over. Michigan had won 35–34. Tom's last game as a Wolverine would be a victory in which Tom gave an awe-

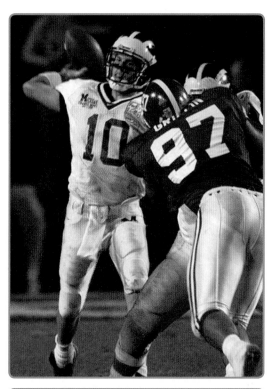

Tom Brady finished his college career with a 35–34 win over the University of Alabama in the Orange Bowl.

some performance. He threw an impressive 369 yards and four touchdown passes.

After all the quarterback controversy and benching and uncertainty, Tom left Michigan a winner. Looking back at his college football years, Tom Brady has said that the whole experience was good for him. It established the will to compete and win as a core part of his character. After going two for two in quarterback competitions, Tom's next stop was the NFL Draft.

3

THE COMEBACK KID

In the NFL, many players hoping to be drafted participate in the NFL **Scouting Combine**. Over the course of one week each spring, players show off their skills, like vertical leap and 40-meter-dash time. At the 2000 Combine, Tom, who was a few weeks away from his college graduation, did not do well. He was never known for being a fast runner or a high jumper. His strengths could not be measured by a stopwatch. Instead, they were on display during a game, when Tom engineered multiple fourth-quarter comebacks in his senior year or rallied his team in his junior year after starting 0–2. There is no Combine statistic called "Leadership."

NFL sportswriters and sportscasters still predicted that Tom would become an NFL quarterback.

They projected that he'd be selected in the second or third round of the draft. Tom's work ethic was becoming well known in pro football circles. And earlier that same year, he had picked apart the famous Alabama defense in the Orange Bowl. Tom and his family were assured that his poor Combine performance would not affect his draft status all that much.

Tom and his family had no idea that after his terrible Combine performance, many teams looked at his scouting report and concluded that Tom wasn't for them. NFL analysts thought he didn't have the right type of physique for the game. They thought he was too skinny and wasn't strong enough. They weren't wrong. Tom was skinny for an NFL quarterback and his 40-yard-dash time was the slowest at the 2000 Draft Combine for quarterbacks. He worked hard to be in the best shape he could be, but he was not a naturally gifted athlete, like many others in the draft.

But what good was being big and fast if the player couldn't lead his team and win? Luckily, someone was asking that question in advance of the draft: Dick Rehbein, the New England Patriots' quarterback coach. Patriots head coach Bill Belichick sent Rehbein to scout out potential quarterbacks. They needed a backup for their current star, Drew Bledsoe. Bledsoe had just turned 28 and had signed a huge $100 million contract. The Patriots weren't looking for the next franchise quarterback. They already had him, but they needed a backup, just in case.

Rehbein went to Ann Arbor to watch Tom Brady play. He returned very excited about the Wolverines' signal-caller and simply told Belichick that Tom Brady was a winner. The Patriots' general manager, Scott Pioli, interviewed Tom at the Combine. He had kind words for the young Wolverine as well. He thought Tom had a confidence that never seemed arrogant. However, the Patriots still were concerned, just like the scouts. But they saw something maybe no one else saw. Jason Licht, a member of the Patriots' staff, pointed out that they weren't setting out to draft a tall, skinny, slow player. They were looking for mental makeup. They wanted a player who could handle pressure and get the win at all costs.

When the draft came around, it was two of the hardest days for Tom and his family. He expected to get drafted on the first day of the draft, in the second or third round. By the end of the first day, 94 players had new NFL teams, 3 of them quarterbacks. Tom was not one of them. Day 2 started the same way. Tom and his family got more and more anxious. Tom's father was stunned. Quarterback after quarterback was called, and with each name, the Brady family became more upset.

Almost 200 names had been called and Tom's wasn't among them. Even the normally cool and collected Tom Brady became anxious. It was getting to the end of the draft, the sixth round. If he was not called soon, he wouldn't be called. But then the call came: Tom was drafted by the New England Patriots. He was the 199th player selected in the 2000 NFL Draft. Six other quarterbacks were picked ahead of him. But none of that mattered. Tom would get his shot. That is all Tom ever needed. In high school and college, he was seen as some team's backup plan. He could do the same in the NFL. All he needed was a chance to show them he was a great quarterback. He knew he could show the world that his physical stature, his 40-meter-dash time—none of that mattered. Being drafted 199th meant one thing—Tom would play like a man who needed to prove himself, just as he always had.

NFL DRAFT

Every year, the NFL teams get to pick new talent to play for them. Eligible players must be at least three years out of high school and have used all their college eligibility. Teams then pick the players, based on the previous season's record. The worst team gets the first pick, the second worst the second pick, and so on. Teams prepare all year to have a good draft strategy to get the players that best fit their team's needs. The draft has seven rounds, with each team getting one pick per round. When it is all said and done, 256 new players are drafted into the NFL. Tom Brady was #199.

Tom's rookie season was exactly what everyone expected. He held a clipboard. Drew Bledsoe started every game. There were good signs for Tom, though. Each NFL team can only have 53 players on its roster. Most football teams only have two or three quarterbacks on their rosters, since there are so many other positions on the team that need to be filled. The Patriots had four quarterbacks, including Tom. Coach Belichick later said he used a roster spot on Brady, knowing he wasn't going to play for the team that year. He just knew Tom was something special and did not want to risk losing him. Tom played 3 minutes and 55 seconds that season and recorded one completed pass for 6 yards in a 34–9 loss to the Detroit Lions. But the big story of that season is that Tom was there. He started as the fourth-string quarterback and showed up to practice every week with his sights on the backup role.

Charlie Weis, the Patriots' offensive coordinator, remembered how hard Tom worked in practice. He recalled how, after practices, even if Tom didn't get a turn playing with the team, he would take the other players who also weren't getting a turn and he would go through the practice script again with them. There were no coaches. It would just be Tom and the other players who were third- or fourth-string.

In 2001, by the end of training camp for his second

season, Tom was the #2 quarterback, right behind Bledsoe. Belichick admitted that, if he had picked his starter on training camp performance alone, Brady would have started over Bledsoe. Tom attributed his success to his experience in college and high school, where he never knew if his spot was assured. So he was always fighting for a job.

At the start of the season, Tom was Bledsoe's backup. He held a clipboard and gave signals. Then the most important play of Tom Brady's career happened, and he wasn't even on the field. In the second game of the season, against the New York Jets, Drew Bledsoe was struggling. It was third down and the Jets had broken up yet another Patriots drive. Drew tried to extend the play. He scrambled to the outside and ran for 8 of the 10 yards they needed to keep the ball. Instead of avoiding the hit, Bledsoe reached forward for the yardage. That is when Mo Lewis, a Pro Bowl linebacker, slammed into him with full force. Bledsoe crumbled under the hit and the ball flew loose and rolled out of bounds. Bledsoe took the field the next set of downs but was having trouble concentrating. He couldn't tell left from right. He had to come out of the game. (Later that night he went to the hospital where doctors discovered that Drew's injury was much worse than the officials thought.)

Belichick had been thinking about starting Brady since the beginning of the season. He even told the Patriots' owner, Robert Kraft, that Brady had the most impressive training camp of anyone he had ever coached. By week 2, with Bledsoe hurt, Belichick did what he had been tempted to do at the start of the season. He sent number 12, Tom Brady, onto the field.

Tom completed five of six passes right away, getting the Patriots to the Jets' 29-yard line. Time was running out and the Jets were up by a touchdown. Tom took three shots at the end zone and missed all three. Tom's time as the #1 quarterback was completely forgettable in that 10–3 loss to the New York Jets, which left the Patriots with an 0–2 record. Most fans, sportswriters, and sports-casters thought that was the end of his season—a short backup stint for the first-string QB, sidelined by a minor injury.

Except the injury wasn't minor. Drew Bledsoe spent four days in the hospital. Doctors told him he could not play for weeks. Everyone else fully expected the job to go back to Bledsoe when he was healthy. Everyone except Tom Brady. The Patriots' cornerback, Ty Law, recalled Tom's confidence. He told Ty, "I'm not giving that job back." Ty thought he was joking.

The next week, Tom was set to start his first NFL

game against the talented Indianapolis Colts, led by a man who would become Tom Brady's fiercest **rival,** Peyton Manning. The Patriots were underdogs in this game. They were starting a second-year backup and outmatched in every position. But there is something to be said for what Tom Brady brings to a team. The Patriots crushed the Colts. Tom Brady threw for just 168 yards and no passing touchdowns, but the people around him played with more energy and heart than Belichick had seen since he took over as head coach. Manning threw three interceptions. Tom threw none. Tom's arm didn't win the game. Tom's leadership did. The Patriots won 44–13 in Tom's first start.

It would be a few more games before everyone would see the Tom Brady that became the face of the Patriots. That happened during his home-game start against the San Diego Chargers. The Chargers' record was 3–1, while the Patriots' was 1–3. The game was filled with mistakes by the Patriots' special teams. A botched **punt** was returned for a touchdown and the normally surefire kicker missed an extra point. Belichick called the performance for the first three quarters the worst he had seen in years.

With less than 9 minutes to go, the Patriots were down 26–16 and fans started heading to the exits. It looked like another lost season for the Patriots. Their star quarterback was injured, and the rest of the team seemed to be falling apart. The fans, the sportswriters, and the sportscasters forgot about Tom Brady's fourth-quarter comebacks in his senior year of college. They must not have seen his overtime win in the Orange Bowl. They probably didn't know that Michigan fans still called him the "Comeback Kid."

Brady started on the Patriots' 26-yard line. He was as cool and collected as any league veteran. Tom drove the team all the way to the San Diego 5-yard line. He used a mix of short and midrange passes and earned five first downs. He went 5 for 8 passing to four different receivers. But the San Diego defense was tough. The Patriots settled for a field goal. They were now within one touchdown of tying the game with only 3:31 left.

The Patriots' defense was also tough. The defense didn't let Doug Flutie and the Chargers' offense get a first down. The Patriots got the ball back in Brady's hands at midfield with 2:10 left. Plenty of time for the Comeback Kid. Tom moved the ball up the field and completed three passes to Troy Brown. A 26-yard pass to Patriots receiver David Patten put them on San Diego's 3-yard line with 36 seconds left. Most teams try to run the ball in when they're this close to their opponent's end zone. Three yards for a professional **running back** should be easy. But the Chargers were known for their amazing defense. Tom faked the run handoff, ran right, and then threw a running pass to a wide-open Jermaine Wiggins for the touchdown. The extra point was good, and the game was tied at 26. It was the Orange Bowl all over again. Tom made it look easy.

The season didn't seem quite so lost. The Patriots were heading to overtime against San Diego. The Chargers got the ball first, but could not get a first down, so they had to punt the ball back to New England. Tom knew he had to get the team close enough to hit a field goal. On the very first play for the Patriots' offense, Tom noticed something. The Chargers were known for their fast and hard defense. Their linebackers were tremendous athletes, who could run down Tom in an instant. All week in practice, Tom was warned by his coach about San Diego's **blitz**. Belichick told him, if you see it, you have to call an **audible**, or a new play. Tom recognized it immediately and shouted out to his teammates.

New play. The line shifted, the receivers ran to their new spots. The defense did not have time to react. Tom hiked the ball and threw it 37 yards downfield to Patten. Then the Chargers made a mistake. Their cornerback grabbed and held Patten while he tried to catch the pass.

That was called **interference**. The Patriots got the ball at the spot of the foul. Brady threw three more complete passes to get the team to the San Diego 26. Belichick knew this was close enough for his kicker, Adam Vinatieri, to seal the game. Adam made the field goal. The Patriots won. Tom completed 33 of 54 passes for 364 yards and two touchdowns, and had no interceptions. It was as if Tom had shouted to the whole world, "I'm not giving this job back!"

The 2001 game against the San Diego Chargers that elevated Tom as the leader and face of the New England Patriots.

4

SUPER TOM

Tom was the starting quarterback for the rest of the season, even after Drew was healthy enough to play. In Belichick's system, there was nothing owed to any players, especially at the most important position on the field—quarterback. Belichick always started whoever he thought was the best player. In this case, Belichick knew Tom was the better QB. Bledsoe had a hard time arguing that fact. After the Chargers game, the team that started 1–3 only lost two more games and went on to end the season 11–5. At the end of the season, Tom had thrown 413 passes and completed 264 of them for 2,843 yards, and 18 touchdowns. The kid from San Mateo who got drafted in the sixth round was picking apart NFL defenses as if he had been doing it his whole life. He played so well, he got his first invite to the **Pro Bowl**. The Comeback Kid took an organization that had only won five games the year before and led them to the playoffs.

Bledsoe remained on the team and took to his new role as Tom's go-to guy. Drew went over plays with him, told him which reads to look out for, and showed him how to be better in the NFL. Drew was like everyone else on that team: he just wanted to win. Unlike Michigan, Tom finally felt that he had some people in his corner. Coach Belichick believed in him. Drew believed in him. His teammates weren't just teammates; they were his friends. On most teams, the players showed up, practiced, showered, and went home. The Patriots were different because, instead of going home after practice, they would all hang out for an hour or so. People credited Tom for this change in dynamic. A lot of the guys on the team were brought in as **free agents**. They were the castoffs from other teams. Just like Tom, they did not have a lot of people in their corner, so they got together and were rooting for each other. Everyone—from practice-squad players and veterans to rookies and players of all races and creeds—was part of the team and everyone hung out together.

THE NFL PLAYOFFS

Every year, the top 12 of the NFL's 32 teams advance to the NFL playoffs. The top teams from each division in each conference go to the playoffs. That makes up 8 of the teams. Then the team with the best remaining record from each conference moves on as well. The tournament is single elimination. Winner advances. Loser goes home. The NFL playoffs have four rounds: wild card, divisional conference, AFC and NFC Conference Championship games, and finally the Super Bowl.

AFC North
Baltimore Ravens
Pittsburgh Steelers
Cincinnati Bengals
Cleveland Browns

NFC North
Green Bay Packers
Chicago Bears
Detroit Lions
Minnesota Vikings

AFC South
Indianapolis Colts
Houston Texans
Tennessee Titans
Jacksonville Jaguars

NFC South
Atlanta Falcons
Carolina Panthers
Tampa Bay Buccaneers
New Orleans Saints

AFC East
New England Patriots
Buffalo Bills
Miami Dolphins
New York Jets

NFC East
New York Giants
Dallas Cowboys
Washington Redskins
Philadelphia Eagles

AFC West
Denver Broncos
Kansas City Chiefs
San Diego Chargers
Oakland Raiders

NFC West
Arizona Cardinals
San Francisco 49ers
Seattle Seahawks
St. Louis Rams

It is a good thing they did, because they would need every single player for what came next. The AFC divisional game against the Oakland Raiders has been called the Snow Bowl, the Tuck Rule game, and, to some fans in the New England area, the start of a dynasty. But no matter who you ask, it was a pivotal game for Tom Brady's career.

You can't control the elements. That was Belichick's advice for his team. Belichick did not know what else to tell them. The snow started long before the game and did not stop. Tom Brady needed a police escort to get to the stadium in time. "Bear with us on the placement of the ball," warned the announcers. The field was covered in snow. They could not see the lines. Players were even having trouble seeing their coaches' calls on the sidelines. Fans at Foxboro Stadium knew they had a sloppy, messy, wet game ahead of them.

Despite the snowstorm and the slick conditions, Tom managed to complete 70 percent of his passes that day. That didn't matter, though. The Patriots went into the fourth quarter down 13–3. Tom got the ball back with 12:29 left in the game. Tom thrived under the pressure. They went to a **no-huddle offense**. Greg Papa, the radio announcer for Raiders' Radio, remembered how good Tom Brady was at the no-huddle, even in the driving snow. Play after play, Tom moved his team down the snow-covered field. He completed nine passes in a row like it was a sunny California day. He took his team from the New England 33 to the Oakland 6-yard line. The Oakland defense had just watched him throw nine precision passes in a row, and they were not going to let him get another. The coverage was tight. Tom could not find an open man, so he faked a pass. The defense bit. Brady ran 6 yards into the end zone. Tom's first playoff touchdown was also his first rushing touchdown. Once again, the "slow runner" from San Mateo brought in the ball by foot. Just like that, the Patriots were back in the game and within a field goal.

Then came one of the most controversial calls in NFL history: the Tuck Rule. It was a play that Patriots fans remember with joy and Raiders fans recall with heartache. The Patriots were down 10–13 and trying to get into field-goal range. Tom dropped back. He did not notice when a

Tom in the infamous AFC division game against the Oakland Raiders known as the Snow Bowl.

Raiders cornerback came out of nowhere, knocking the ball loose into the fresh snow. A Raiders player fell on the ball. As far as anyone knew, that was it. The game was over. Raiders fans throughout the country celebrated and Patriots fans started heading to the exits. But it wasn't over after all. The officials reviewed the replay. Tom's arm was moving forward when he was hit. They ruled that it wasn't a fumble at all, but an incomplete pass. To this day, ask any Raiders fans, and they will tell you how vehemently they disagree. But the refs got it right. The rulebook explicitly stated that a forward motion, even if the quarterback is "tucking" the ball back into his body, was an incomplete pass and not a fumble. The rule was changed a few years later. The very next play, Brady completed a 13-yard pass to Patten, putting the Patriots in field-goal range. Vinatieri came out and hit another clutch field goal to tie the game.

The game went into overtime. Anyone who's seen the Comeback Kid, Tom Brady, play knew that was a mere formality. The Patriots got the ball first. Tom completed eight of eight passes, driving the team up the field and into field-goal range. At that time, NFL rules stated that the first team to score in overtime won. The team was close enough to hit a field goal under normal conditions, but Belichick wanted insurance in the driving snow and wind.

He asked Tom to go for it on 4th and 4. Tom dropped back and his offensive line gave him plenty of time. He looked to his left and saw David Patten free. Tom threw the ball to Patten as the receiver slipped in the snow. From his knees, Patten reached up, and caught the pass for a 6-yard gain and a first down. The Patriots' running back kept things moving with another 8-yard run. Tom and his team got all the way to the 5-yard line. Vinatieri cleared the snow off the ground to make room for the holder. Adam got a clean snap, a good hold. The ball sailed through the still-falling snow through the goalpost. The game was over. The Patriots and Tom Brady were heading to the AFC Championship. Tom ended the game with 32 completed passes in blizzard conditions and another come-from-behind, fourth-quarter victory.

The AFC Championship was Tom's biggest stage yet. The ragtag Patriots were one game away from the Super Bowl. Once again, they were underdogs. The Pittsburgh Steelers were a powerhouse. The Patriots were a fluke. But the Pats were winning, and analysts weren't quite sure how. The experts' stat sheets did not have a column for heart, as Tom's father had said. They would need plenty of heart and grit to advance to the Super Bowl. The Steelers had the #1 defense in the NFL.

Tom played spectacularly through nearly the first two quarters of the game. He completed 12 of 18 passes and the Patriots were up 7–3, thanks to a highlight-reel 55-yard punt return from Troy Brown. Just after the two-minute warning, Tom was in a 3rd-and-long situation. He dropped back and the pocket was starting to collapse. Just as he always did, Tom stood tall and delivered a pass over the middle to a streaking Troy Brown, who took it 27 yards. Tom was prepared to get hit, but the defensive back went low. He got Tom bent around. Tom had trouble standing up. He grabbed his ankle. He limped to the sideline. Belichick turned to Bledsoe. It was his turn to keep this storybook season going.

Bledsoe was without a doubt the best backup quarterback in the league. No one on the Steelers' sideline was excited to see him. He quickly moved the ball up the field. With less than 2 minutes left, he hit Patten three times; the last one was an 11-yard strike in the end zone. The seven-point underdog Patriots never gave up that lead. They finished the game in a huge upset, 24–17. The top-ranked Steelers fell to a team that no one saw making the playoffs. Now Tom and his merry band of misfits were heading to the Super Bowl.

The Patriots were ready to face the "Greatest Show on

Turf," also known as the St. Louis Rams. The Rams were led by two-time league MVP Kurt Warner and had the top-ranked offense in all of football. They led in passing yards, passes completed, passing touchdowns, rushing touch-downs, and yards per catch. They had won the Super Bowl two years earlier and were the favorites to do it again. No one expected Tom and the Patriots' Cinderella story to challenge the Rams, who were 14–2. No one was picking the Patriots to win. Some even predicted a blowout. An underdog can only get lucky so many times. Everyone still thought it was just luck and not heart.

While the sportswriters and sportscasters chattered, Belichick was preparing his team for the biggest game of their lives. Belichick drilled and drilled with his team on how to contain the Rams' offense just enough to give Tom a chance. His ankle was healed up and he was set to start. Belichick made it simple for Tom. Read your coverage, go through your progressions, and make the throw. The defense will worry about making sure you don't have to do too much.

They went out as a team and worked their game plan. The defense stopped Marshall Faulk, the St. Louis run-ning back, throughout the game. Ty Law picked off a pass from Kurt Warner for a touchdown. On the offensive end, Tom was calm and methodical. He realized that it was just another game. With 1 minute and 20 seconds left in the first half, Tom drove the team down the field after a fumble recovery. On the Rams' 8-yard line with 31 seconds left in the half, Tom dropped back. Patten was heading for the back corner of the end zone. Tom threw a fast spiral to the perfect spot, above the head of the defender, but right into the hands of a diving David Patten. Touchdown Patriots!

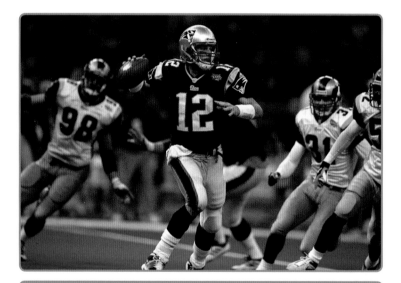

Tom in Super Bowl XXXVI against the St. Louis Rams. The underdog Patriots beat the Rams on a field goal with seconds remaining.

Tom and company went to halftime up 14–3. It was the most the Greatest Show on Turf had been down all year.

The Patriots were up 17–3 going into the fourth quarter. Everyone knew the legendary Rams offense could not be held forever, and the Rams scored two quick touchdowns. The upset was slipping away from the Patriots. If the Rams' offense got going, the Patriots were in trouble. Conventional wisdom said that the Patriots, who were out of time-outs, should take a knee and take it to overtime. Offensive coordinator Charlie Weis wanted to take a shot.

Weis knew they had the momentum. He decided to just go for it. This was welcome news to Tom. Tom Brady did his best work with time winding down and the game on the line. Weis instructed him to make a play if there was an open receiver near the sidelines. Otherwise, Tom was instructed to throw the checkdown and run out the clock. Tom turned to Drew Bledsoe. Drew had become a bit of a mentor to him. The starter-turned-backup looked Tom in the eye and said, "Just sling it."

Tom started the drive by doing exactly what Weis asked. He threw a few passes, got a first down, and spiked the ball to stop the clock. He hit J. R. Redmond on another short pass that was extended to 11 yards. Tom spiked the ball again to stop the clock with 33 seconds left. Tom called the play "64 Max All In." He took the direct snap, dropped back, and threw it over the middle to a crossing Troy Smith for 23 yards. Tom quickly went up to the line and threw one more quick pass to his tight end, Jermaine

Wiggins, for 6 more yards. He spiked the ball with 7 seconds left. Tom got them all the way to the St. Louis 30-yard line. Once again, as he had done all season, Tom left it up to his kicker to seal it. Veteran announcer John Madden admitted that what the young kid Tom Brady did gave him goose bumps.

Adam Vinatieri ran onto the field. The tension on the sideline was overwhelming. Adam hit 48-yard field goals all the time in practice, but never to win a Super Bowl. Everyone on the Patriots' sideline held their breath. The kick was up and it sailed dead center through the uprights as time expired. The 14-point underdogs beat the St. Louis Rams to win Super Bowl XXXVI and the championship for the 2001 season. The announcers could not believe it. New England had the best team in all of football. It was New England's first-ever Super Bowl win.

Tom Brady was named Super Bowl MVP for his game-winning performance. The kid from San Mateo stood in front of 50,000-plus people. The sixth-round draft afterthought had gone from fourth-string quarterback to Super Bowl MVP in less than two years. He looked out over the stands with thousands of cheering fans chanting his name. He just shook his head in disbelief. He was a Super Bowl champion.

5

ALMOST PERFECT

The Comeback Kid was earning new nicknames, like Tom Terrific and Tommy Touchdown. Tom was now the face of the Patriots franchise. They were no longer known as lovable losers, but a dynasty in the making. The season following the Super Bowl, the team had a 9–7 record, good enough for second place in the AFC East, but missed the playoffs. Belichick and Pioli traded Drew Bledsoe to the Buffalo Bills, essentially telling Tom that he was the future. Tom took that seriously, but a shoulder injury prevented him from playing to his full potential. Tom was still able to throw an NFL-high 28 touchdown passes. It was just not enough to win the AFC East. Chad Pennington, drafted 181 spots ahead of Tom, would take his New York Jets to the playoffs instead. Tom had the long off-season to think about what he could do to help the team in the future. He would never miss the playoffs again.

In 2003, Tom Brady came back ready to work. The team started 2–2, but went on to win their final 12 games in a row. Tom finished third in MVP voting behind Peyton Manning and Steve McNair. The team dominated through the playoffs, beating the Tennessee Titans and running circles around Peyton Manning's Colts. The Patriots intercepted Manning four times. Manning had lost 10 of the first 12 games he played against Brady.

The Patriots made it to the Super Bowl again. This time they faced the Carolina Panthers. It was as if they had recycled the script from a previous movie to make its sequel. The score was close down the stretch. The game was tied at 29 with just over 1 minute left in the fourth quarter, just the way Tom liked it. He took advantage of a botched punt and moved the Patriots within field-goal range in just a few passes. He threw for a completion then stopped the clock at 9 seconds. It felt like a rerun of Super Bowl XXXVI, against the Rams. Vinatieri came out, nailed the field goal, and the New England Patriots were champions again! Tom was the Super Bowl MVP once more, with 354 yards passing and three touchdowns.

Brady came back and started the 2004 season undefeated through six games. The Patriots' 21 straight regular-season and postseason victories is the longest winning streak ever in NFL history and is enshrined in the Football Hall of Fame. The Patriots ended the season 14–2, again behind Brady's Pro Bowl–earning 28 touchdown passes. On top of the Pro Bowl, *The Sporting News* named Tom Brady the Sportsman of the Year. Brady once again rolled through the playoffs, beating Manning's Colts 20–3 and the Steelers 41–27. Tom threw five touchdowns and no interceptions in those playoffs. They made quick work of the Eagles at the Super Bowl. They did not need a fourth-quarter field goal from Vinatieri. At only age 27, Tom Brady, the player most scouts thought would never play in the NFL, was now a three-time Super Bowl champion.

THE NFL PLAYOFFS

Games started: 41
Record: 30–11
Pass Completion Percentage: 63.0
Quarterback Rating: 89.8
Yards: 11,388
Touchdowns: 73

After three championships in four years, the Patriots were considered the team to beat. No one knew that Tom Brady's best season was yet to come. They had to wait a few years, until 2007, when the Patriots brought in big-name receivers for Tom to throw to. Wes Welker came to them from Miami and Randy Moss out of Oakland. Moss even took a huge pay cut to get a chance to be Tom Brady's #1 receiver! He knew that working with Brady would mean a chance to make history. At only 30 years old, there were whispers that Tom Brady might end up being the greatest of all time, but it was not until the 2007 season that people began to take those rumors seriously.

No one was quite sure what Belichick and Scott Pioli were up to. They brought in three skilled receivers for Tom, but no one understood just how it would all click together. There had never been an offense like it. This experiment would become the all-time greatest offense in history. Today, it is the offense every team looks to as a model. Cameron Worrell, who played safety for the Miami Dolphins that year, said that in meetings to review game tapes coaches were telling them about the Patriots' no-huddle offense and three or four receivers. It was a first of its kind, but it has since become a standard in the NFL: the **spread offense**. The offense was designed to make a defense pick their poison: stay home and give up the deep ball, or chase the deep ball and have Wes Welker burn you over the middle from the slot. Defenses struggled to figure it out. The no-huddle, fast play, with Tom calling plays on the field, left defenses gasping for breath.

SPREAD OFFENSE

The legendary 2007 Patriots offense was a variation of the spread offense that was already seen in college games. The idea of the spread offense was simple: spread out the defense. The formations included four and five receivers, requiring the defense to be spread from sideline to sideline. This opened up routes that were much harder than before. Since 2007, the spread offense has become common in the NFL, but defensive coordinators have reacted, adding smaller, quicker defenders who can keep up with the glut of receivers.

The Patriots' success wasn't simply a matter of scheme and talent. It stemmed from a great deal of hard work. Tom and Randy spent a lot of time working together to get things just right. According to Moss, they clicked instantly. Moss spent hours preparing with Brady, talking about protections and audibles. Both players wanted to master the playbook and sync up their plays as best they could. Moss wanted to know what Brady was thinking at all times. Every record they set was all because of this hard work and the strong bond between the two players.

The Patriots' young offensive coordinator, Josh McDaniels, also worked hard to get all the new receivers on board with this game-changing new system. Josh was 31, only one year older than Brady, but Belichick trusted him to guide this offense, which would sent shock waves through the NFL. Every single player needed to keep his head up because Tom was going to spread the ball around. Any eligible receiver on the field could get the ball thrown on a rope to him at any time. The scheme seems obvious now, but it was one of a kind in 2007. It was also a perfect system for Tom Brady, a quarterback who was cool and calm in every game situation and at every speed. Football could not move too fast for him. Randy Moss warned the local sportswriters and sportscasters on his first call as a Patriot that they were going to see things they had never seen before.

It was true. No one had ever seen an offense this efficient. No one had ever seen defenses this frustrated. The first game of the season was against Chad Pennington and the New York Jets. Tom threw 22 completions on 28 attempts for 297 yards and three touchdowns, including a 51-yard bomb to Randy Moss. Moss caught nine passes for 183 yards. The Patriots easily won 38–14. It wouldn't even be close to their most lopsided win of the season.

As the season went on, the numbers kept piling up. The Patriots averaged 37 points a game during the season. By the time the season was over, they were the only team in history to go 16–0 and just the third to have an undefeated season. Their offense was like nothing anyone had ever seen and it's never been seen since. John Madden described it as the best offense he had ever seen. He thought Tom Brady was playing quarterback better than any player he'd seen in his decades in football.

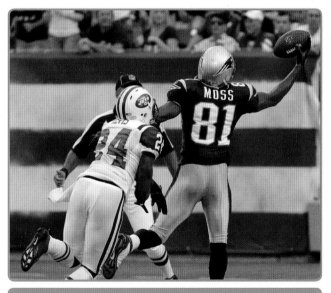

Randy Moss making a one-handed grab against the New York Jets.

The Patriots' offense scored 589 total points, outscoring the Rams' Greatest Show on Turf by 33 points. New England had the highest-scoring offense in history. Tom threw a league-record 50 touchdown passes that season, and was only picked off eight times. Randy Moss had the most TD catches that season with 23 and Wes Welker tied the most receptions for the season with 112 receptions. If there was a record, this team broke it. Tom Brady was voted the league MVP, his first time receiving that honor. He got all but 1 of the 50 MVP votes available in 2007. He was also named AFC Offensive Player of the Week seven times, Associated Press (AP) Offensive Player of the Year, and AP Male Athlete of the Year. He wasn't the only one to haul home a bunch of hardware. Randy Moss earned a few Offensive Player of the Week awards and Belichick walked away with AP Coach of the Year. While all these accolades were great, Tom Brady and the Patriots had their sights on one piece of hardware in particular. They wanted to go to Super Bowl XLII and win the Lombardi Trophy again.

The playoffs would be much harder than the regular season. Teams had all season to study the Patriots' tapes and adjust for this new circus of an offense. The AFC Divisional Round against the Jacksonville Jaguars was tight for the first half. The teams entered the second half tied at 14. Tom played spectacularly, not throwing an incompletion until well into the third quarter. He ended the game 26 for 28. The third quarter is when the Patriots' fast play finally wore down the strong Jacksonville defense. Tom marched his team down the field and got them to the 6-yard line. They ran a play where Tom faked a high snap and handoff to Faulk. The defense bit on it and left Tom wide open with the football. He threw a short pass to Welker in the end zone, right between two unsuspecting defenders. The Patriots were up 21–14 and they never looked back. They won the game 31–20. Welker caught nine passes and a touchdown. The offense was still clicking.

The next game was the AFC title game, against the San Diego Chargers. It was the New England defense who won the game. The Patriots' offense struggled at times, with Tom throwing three interceptions. It wouldn't matter because the defense did not give up a single touchdown, only four field goals. The Patriots won 21–12, thanks to two passing TDs from Tom. With that victory, the Patriots were the first team to ever go 18–0. They were one win away from the perfect season and they were the heavy favorites to beat the New York Giants in Super Bowl XLII.

At first the Super Bowl, which everyone expected to

be a clash of two offensive powerhouses, was instead a defensive slugfest. The score at the half was 7–3. The Giants' game plan was simple. The Patriots' offense required what is called an "empty set." That meant that all available positions were out to receive passes. There would always be one defensive player unblocked. It was up to Tom to get the ball off before that defender could get to him. It worked out well in the regular season, but the Giants' defensive front was too fast. Michael Strahan, the star Giants defensive end, said that if they did not get to Brady and put him on his butt, they wouldn't stand a chance. They got to him. Tom was sacked five times.

Even though Tom spent a lot of the game on his back, he kept getting up and moving the ball. With 7:54 left in the game, Tom had the team in a position to win. Tom engineered a 5-minute drive where he completed eight passes to Welker, Moss, and Faulk. He drove 80 yards. The team was down 7–10. On the 6-yard line, Tom dropped back and threw to Moss, who had gotten away from his defender, Giants cornerback Corey Webster. Randy caught it easily, as if he and Tom were playing catch in the driveway. The Patriots were up 14–10 with only 2:42 to go. Eli Manning would need a miracle to break up the perfect season.

The Patriots' defense played conservatively. They just needed to avoid the big play. Brandon Jacobs, the Giants running back, picked up a few yards, but the Giants were held up at their own 44. Third down and 5 with 1:15 remaining. If they stopped Eli Manning here, the game was over and they would be the first team in history to have a perfect 19–0 season. The ball was snapped and Eli's pocket collapsed. The Patriots' pass rushers had their hands on Eli. They just needed to get him down for the sack to secure the win. Jarvis Green had Eli's jersey. He pulled at it, but somehow Eli shook him away, stepped forward, and threw up high and far away. The ball did not seem intended for anyone in particular and it came down right on top of wide receiver David Tyree's head. Tyree grabbed the ball with one hand and pressed it against his helmet as he was pulled to the ground. He kept the ball from touching the ground and secured it. It was a catch. The "Helmet Catch" is remembered to this day as one of the most miraculous plays in Super Bowl history. Two plays later, the Giants scored a touchdown pass to win. The Giants needed a miracle and they got one. The Patriots ended their near-perfect season 18–1.

Tom Brady said in the documentary *Tom versus Time*, that he still has trouble watching the replay of that catch. The team's record-setting year was all wasted.

Tom may have walked away with the MVP Award and other honors, but he had also lost on the biggest stage. Tom had never lost a Super Bowl. Tom hated losing. He vowed to be back.

Tom and the New England Patriots suffered a 17–14 loss to the New York Giants in Super Bowl XLII.

6

DOWN BUT NOT OUT

Tom was hoping to use the 2008 season to improve on the Patriots' near-perfect 2007 season. They had many of the same personnel and coaching staff. He still had Moss and Welker. The New England squad was an early favorite in the AFC again. But all that changed in the first quarter of the first game against the Kansas City Chiefs. Seven minutes in and the season was over for Tom. One of Kansas City's safeties hit Tom low on the pass rush. Tom's knee buckled and he hit the ground, unable to stand back up. His scream could be heard from the sidelines. Everyone knew what had happened. Tom tore the ACL and the MCL in his left knee—the type of injury that requires several surgeries and takes an entire year of recovery. Tom had to hand over the reins to his backup, Matt Cassel.

Matt had not started a game since he was in high school, but Josh McDaniels, New England's offensive coordinator, was able to draw up genius plays for him. The Patriots went 11 and 5 without Tom, but did not make the playoffs. Tom spent the year recovering, and so did the Patriots. The season was a loss, but Tom would be back. He approached his rehab with the same zeal and intensity he brought to football practice. He said it helped him realize how fragile his career was. Sitting on the sidelines for an entire season just reminded Tom how much he loved playing the game. It made him realize that at any point his career could be over, so he'd better enjoy it. Unlike Bledsoe, so many years earlier, Tom Brady did not have to worry about his backup taking his job. Robert Kraft, the Patriots owner, even told Tom they hoped he'd be the starting quarterback for another 10 years.

INJURY REHAB

Tom injured the ACL and MCL ligaments in his left knee. A ligament is a band of tissue that holds two bones together. These ligaments are what make your elbows, knees, and other joints bend. The ACL and MCL make the knee bend. If you can't bend your knee, you can't play football. Tom needed to undergo two surgeries over the course of a year before he was able to run and throw again.

In 2009, Tom returned to the lineup. Cassel was traded after his serviceable season. Tom was the Patriots quarterback. He put together another 10-win season and won the NFL's Comeback Player of the Year Award, which is given to players who return to the league with extraordinary performances. His numbers that season were classic Brady: 28 touchdowns; a 65 percent rate of completed passes; and a division title. Still, the Patriots weren't playing their best, and they fell behind in their only playoff game that year. They lost to the Ravens 33–14.

The next year Tom earned his first unanimous MVP Award, partly thanks to the Patriots' new strategy. In the second round of the 2010 NFL Draft, they selected tight end Rob Gronkowski, better known as Gronk. He would quickly become one of Tom's all-time favorite receivers. Bill Belichick centered his new offense on the tight-end players. Belichick believed that was the hardest position after quarterback. He knew that opposing teams' defense reacted to where the tight end lined up. Tight ends get shuffled all over the place, unlike other receiver positions like **wide receivers**, or **wideouts**, or running backs. They are also expected to be as good at blocking as a lineman and as good at catching passes as a wide receiver.

Belichick thought Gronk had a great football mind. Brady agreed, but the quarterback also thought Gronkowski needed some seasoning. The way Rob tells it, Tom was mean to him. He eventually realized that Tom was the team's leader and he saw real potential in Rob. Rob came to see Tom as a teacher. He could be hard on Rob, but Tom wanted Gronkowski to learn the game and become a better football player.

Over time, Rob became Tom's favorite target. In Gronk's rookie year, Tom threw to him 59 times, with Rob hauling in 42 of them for 10 touchdowns. The next season, Tom and Rob really started to click. Tom threw 17 touchdowns to Rob in the 2011 season. In the AFC Divisional Round, against the Denver Broncos, Tom connected with Rob for 10 receptions and three touchdowns, to win the game 45–10. It seemed like nothing could stop the veteran QB and his fiery young tight end.

After the Patriots won the AFC Championship Game against the Baltimore Ravens 23–20, Tom ran into an old foe at Super Bowl XLVI: Eli Manning and the New York Giants. The Giants controlled the pace of the game, which featured more field goals than touchdowns. Rob only caught two passes. Tom played well. He even engineered a Super Bowl–record 96-yard touchdown drive, but it was not enough. Eli Manning, the Patriot Slayer, struck again, and Tom lost his second Super Bowl to the same man, this time by a 21–17 score.

Tom was determined to avenge his two losses and win another Super Bowl. He would not return to the Super Bowl for another three seasons. The year 2014 was a vintage Tom Brady season. He led his team to a 12–4 record. Tom spread the ball around, with seven different receivers recording TD catches. When Wes Welker left to play elsewhere, Julian Edelman stepped up. He ran similar short, quick routes with a team-high 92 catches. But it was Rob Gronkowski who was Tom's favorite receiver

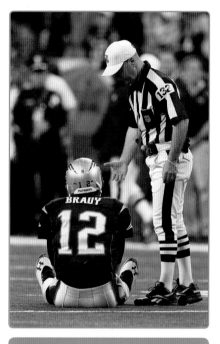

The New England Patriots lost to the New York Giants a second time in Super Bowl XLVI.

in the **red zone**, the last 20 yards before the end zone. Rob recorded a team-high 12 touchdowns on the season. Tom had a way of finding Rob, who used his huge stature to reach over defenders. Or Brady would pass to Gronkowski, who would lower his shoulder and bowl over opponents.

After a close 35–31 game with the Ravens in the divisional round, the Patriots toppled the Colts 45–7. Their new quarterback, Andrew Luck, had trouble against the Patriots and only completed 12 of 33 passes for no touchdowns. And Tom was terrific again, throwing three touchdowns. However, the real story of this game would not come out until a year later and it would have less to do with how well Tom threw the ball, than with the balls themselves. (More on that later.)

Tom and his new squad were heading to the Super Bowl for his sixth time, an NFL record. When Tom looked around the locker room, he didn't see anyone from his first Super Bowl win in 2001 or his last one in 2004. Each guy currently on the team came to the Patriots with Tom as their quarterback and the leader of the team. This was the team that he had helped build with Bill Belichick. Tom was ready to win his fourth Super Bowl, where he'd be going up against the Seattle Seahawks.

Super Bowl XLIX was held in the University of Phoenix Stadium in Arizona. Tom knew it better as the building where Eli Manning and the New York Giants ruined his perfect season. There were a lot of bad memories for Tom in that building, and he was ready to fill it with good ones.

The score went back and forth for the whole first half. At halftime the score was tied 14–14. But after a disastrous third quarter, the Patriots were down 24–14, going into the fourth quarter. No team had ever come back from a deficit of 10 or more in the fourth quarter to win the Super Bowl. But that's the thing about Tom Brady: he specializes in fourth-quarter comebacks.

Getting the ball back early in the fourth quarter, Tom put together a series of improbable passes for long gains. Tom completed five of seven passes and marched 68 yards into the Seahawks' end zone. He once again found his wide receiver at the back of the end zone for the 6-yard strike. It was now a three-point ball game.

The Patriots' defense stood strong, and Tom took over on his own 32 with 6:52 remaining. He ate up more than 4 minutes on the play clock to move his team into scoring range. On the next play, Tom spotted his receiver, Julian Edelman, and threw right to him at the corner of the end zone. Tom turned to his sideline, pointed at his coach, and pumped his fist. They'd done it again!

But there were still slightly more than 2 minutes left (2:02, to be precise). The Patriots' defense now had to stop the great Seattle offense. Their third-year quarterback, Russell Wilson, moved his team down the field in 2 minutes. Before long the Seahawks were on the 5-yard line with a first down and plenty of time. But when Wilson attempted to pass the ball, Patriots cornerback Malcolm Butler jumped the route and came down with the ball for one of the most memorable interceptions in Super Bowl history. The game was over. New England had won 28–24. Tom Brady had waited six years to be crowned a champion in that building. Once again, the Patriots were the world's best football team.

The Patriots' offensive line gave Tom plenty of time to throw in New England's Super Bowl XLIX victory.

7

THE BRADY DYNASTY

Tom Brady was not allowed to enjoy his fourth Super Bowl win too much. Why? Mostly because of a 243-page report, called "Investigative Report Concerning Footballs Used During the AFC Championship Game on January 18, 2015." It may sound boring, but it was the biggest story in football in almost two years. Here's a much shorter version. The Colts noticed that some of the footballs they were using in the AFC Championship Game were under-inflated. They reported that to the NFL. The NFL concluded that the Patriots' equipment managers had let air out of the balls to make them easier to grip, throw, and catch. The NFL could not prove this assertion, but league officials were fairly certain that Tom Brady either knew about the underinflated balls and told no one, or, even worse, had instructed the equipment managers to do it. The league suspended Brady for four games.

To this day Brady maintains his innocence. He even went to court to defend himself. While the court was hearing the case, his suspension was put on hold. Tom could play the 2015 season. The season was mostly forgettable. The Patriots lost in the first round of the playoffs after Edelman and Gronk suffered injuries. The sportswriters and sportscasters were still fixated on what they called "Deflategate."

Over the course of the year, the case kept going to higher courts as Tom Brady and his team appealed the suspension. On July 13, 2016, the federal appeals court finally ruled against Brady's appeal. Tom was done fighting. He maintained his innocence but was tired of the media distraction. He would serve his four-game suspension at the start of the 2016 season.

Brady's fans blamed the NFL commissioner for what they felt was unfair treatment of Tom Brady and the Patriots organization. "Free Brady" became a rallying call for New England sports fans. The season was no longer about just winning games but about getting "revenge." Tom was a bit less dramatic about it when asked. "I've tried to just be as positive as I can be. I think that's kind of always been my motto. I know over the course of my career, I've been faced with different things and I've tried to overcome them the best way I could or the best I knew how. I'll try to do the same thing."

The Patriots entered the start of the 2016 season with 18 players who were not on their championship 2015 roster. And for the first time since 2008, their starter would not be Tom Brady, but instead third-year quarterback, Jimmy Garoppolo. Jimmy played the best you could expect in that scenario. In fact, of the four Brady-less games, Jimmy won the first of them. Jimmy looked confident and poised in the pocket. A little of Tom had rubbed off on him. But the season kept getting weirder when Jimmy was hit hard by Miami tackle Kiko Alonso. Jimmy hurt his shoulder. He could not play. Now, the third-string quarterback, rookie Jacoby Brissett, was in the game. If the young Brissett felt out of his element, he didn't show it. He led the Patriots to a 31–24 win. The Patriots went into the third game with Brissett as the starter, and he put together a 27–0 blowout of the Houston Texans. The fourth game was the hard one. Brissett was banged up and the Patriots did not have a backup quarterback left. Wide receiver Julian Edelman even took a few plays at quarterback. They lost the game 16–0. Asked after the game about Brady's return, Edelman said he was excited to get his quarterback back.

When Tom came back for his first NFL game of the season, he crushed the Cleveland Browns for 406 yards passing. Many Patriots fans traveled all the way to Cleveland to see the return of their hero. After the game, Tom did not want to talk about Commissioner Roger Goodell or his suspension. Instead, he wanted to talk about the fans. "I think we've got the best fans in the world. They showed up today and it was great to hear them."

The Patriots ended the season 14–2. Tom completed 67 percent of his passes for 28 touchdowns in only 12 games. He only threw two interceptions, which is still the greatest touchdown-to-interception ratio in history. He earned a 112 **passer rating**, the second highest of his career after 2007. Tom was ready for the playoffs.

In the first round, the Patriots went up against the Houston Texans. The Texans had the best defense in the league, led by defensive powerhouse J. J. Watt. Tom struggled at points in the game, more than he had all season, but the Patriots never trailed. Despite getting banged up a bit, they walked away with a 34–16 victory. The AFC Championship was against a familiar foe, Ben Roethlisberger and the Pittsburgh Steelers. Tom just didn't lose to them. Tom had won the past six of seven matchups with the Steelers. Even Steelers safety Mike Mitchell had to admit that Tom Brady was probably the G.O.A.T.

Just as Brady had done time and time again, he wiped the floor with the Steelers, 36–17. He threw three touchdowns for 384 yards and never looked back. Redemption was waiting for him at Super Bowl LI at NRG Stadium in Houston, with only the Atlanta Falcons standing in the Patriots' way.

Most Patriots fans probably won't watch the first three quarters of Super Bowl LI again, and for good reason. The Patriots entered the fourth quarter down 28–3. No team had ever come back from a deficit that big in the Super Bowl. They were going to need more than a miracle. They were going to need each other. With Tom's leadership, no one ever felt out of it. Coming back from 25 points down would be a hard thing to do, but with the right team and the right leader, anything could happen.

Going into the fourth quarter, the G.O.A.T. had only thrown one pass that went for a touchdown; unfortunately, it was to Falcons cornerback Robert Alford. It would make sense for fans to turn off the game. But something clicked late in the third. Edelman credits conditioning. He says Belichick and Tom would run them up "the hill" every day after practice, no matter how grueling. So by the fourth quarter, the Falcons were gassed and tired, but the Patriots were ready to run up the hill.

In the third quarter, down by 25, Tom drove the team

as he always did. They went 75 yards for the score and used up 6 minutes off the clock. The kicker missed the extra point, but that was fine. He made up for it by capping another 6-minute drive by the Patriots with a field goal: the score was now 28–12. They were finally moving the ball. On the next possession, Matt Ryan, called Matty Ice for his cool demeanor in big games, fumbled the ball on a sack. Tom got the ball on the Atlanta 25. Tom hit four passes in a row. The final one was to Danny Amendola, a route he had run a million times. He ran to the end zone, and then cut his route to the outside. His defender just lost him. Tom hit him from the short drop back for the score. Tom wasted no time. He put two fingers in the air, signaling to everyone in the stadium that they were going for two. They didn't do anything fancy. The running back James White just took it straight up the middle. Score now: 28–20. It was suddenly a one-TD football game with 5:56 minutes left in the game.

After a brief possession of the ball by the Falcons, the Patriots got the ball back with 3:30. That is almost too much time for Tom. During the drive, the Patriots finally got their own impossible catch. After watching the Helmet Catch almost 10 years earlier, it was their turn for some good fortune. Julian Edelman had a step on Robert Alford from the right slot over the middle. Tom threw the pass, but somehow Alford closed on Edelman. He got a hand on the ball and batted it up in the air. Edelman knew not to give up on the play and dove after it, along with three other Falcons defenders. After bouncing the ball around, Edelman managed to gain control just before the ball touched the ground. A video review confirmed Edelman's reception. After juggling the ball in the air like a circus act, Edelman caught the ball for a 23-yard grab. First down Patriots. Tom completed the next three passes to get his team on the 1-yard line. Once again, the Patriots kept it simple. James White blasted it in over the right guard with 57 seconds left.

Tom signaled with two fingers that they were going for a two-point conversion again. The whole game, the whole season, and, in some way, the Brady Dynasty, relied on this

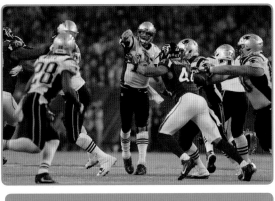

Tom led the Patriots to a 34–28 overtime victory over the Atlanta Falcons in Super Bowl LI.

play. Lined up on the 2-yard line, Brady dropped back quickly and quickly passed to a fast-moving Amendola, who made it into the end zone. The game was tied 28–28. They headed to overtime.

The Patriots won the coin toss and Tom drove his team down the field with mechanical precision. Completing his first five passes to get them on the Atlanta 2-yard line. On second down, James White crashed into the Falcons' end zone. The Comeback Kid did it again, winning Super Bowl LI by a score of 34–28. Tom Brady has his fifth Super Bowl ring. The sixth-round, 199th draft pick now was tied for the most NFL championships with the legendary Bart Starr. He held almost every Super Bowl record possible. The kid from San Mateo was the Greatest of All Time.

Tom celebrating his fifth Super Bowl victory.

8

THE G.O.A.T.

Tom Brady tied or surpassed almost every quarterback record in the NFL. He turned 40 right before the start of the 2017 season. He spent the off-season dealing with rumors. Some sportswriters and sports broadcasters were sure he was going to retire. He was already one of the oldest players in the NFL. He had a wife and family at home. Tom was the quarterback of the reigning Super Bowl champion team. His claim to Greatest of All Time was already strong. No one would be surprised if he ended his career. But in August, just las he had for the previous 16 years, Tom was back in a Patriots uniform, ready to start a new season.

Most players who won the Super Bowl the year before were still with the Patriots. They played as if they had not missed a day. The team finished the season with 13 wins and only 3 losses. Tom played his best season of football in years. He threw 4,577 yards—the most yards in the entire league. He threw 32 touchdowns and was only intercepted eight times. He continued his habit of throwing to his big tight end, Rob Gronkowski. Gronk scored 8 touchdowns and had 69 receptions, the most on the team. Tom's statistics were eye-popping. Once again, he was named Most Valuable Player. With three MVP titles, he is tied for second most in league history (Peyton Manning has five). He was also the oldest MVP ever at 40 years old.

Tom Brady and the New England Patriots played such a great regular season, they went into the playoffs as a favorite to win the Super Bowl. It seemed as if nothing could slow down Brady. After a first bye week, Tom went right back to work against the Tennessee Titans. The Patriots started the game down by 7 after the Titans' rookie wide receiver caught a one-handed pass in the end zone. Tom quickly answered with a score of his own. At the end of a long drive, Tom threw one of the easiest passes of his career. From about 3 feet away, Tom threw a short, underhanded pass to James White, who ran 6 yards for a touchdown. The Patriots wouldn't trail again. The Patriots won 35–14. Tom threw for 337 yards and 3 touchdowns. The second touchdown was his 553rd career touchdown pass, which moved him to second all-time, ahead of Brett Favre. This game also marked his 10th playoff game with 3 or more touchdown passes. This gave him the NFL record, surpassing Joe Montana's 9 three-touchdown games. One more record belonged to Tom.

The next game pitted the Pats against the Jacksonville Jaguars for the AFC Championship. The winner would play in the Super Bowl. The Patriots were in trouble before the game even started. In practice during the week before the game, Tom got his hand hurt during drills with a running back. His throwing hand had a large gash on it and some sportswriters and sports broadcasters thought he might not be able to play. But Tom Brady fought through the pain and showed up ready to play. The Jaguars had a big and fast defense that gave the Patriots trouble during the game. Making things worse, Rob Gronkowski was injured as a result of an illegal hit in the second quarter. Tom had to play most of the game without his favorite target and with a hurt hand. The Patriots came into the fourth quarter down 20–10. A lot of quarterbacks would have gotten nervous or failed with so many things going against them. Not Tom Brady. He was the Comeback Kid, after all.

With 12 minutes left in the game, Tom put together an 85-yard touchdown drive with several long passes of 31 yards, 21 yards, and 18 yards. It took Tom 3 minutes and 19 seconds to bring them within 3 points, 20–17. After that, both defenses played extremely well, so neither offense could put together scoring plays. Then the Patriots defense pinned the Jaguars near their own end zone. And after a bad punt, Tom and the offense got the ball at the Jaguars' 30-yard line. Tom didn't have far to go to take the lead. With five plays and a short 4-yard pass to the back of the end zone, the Patriots took their first lead of the game with 3 minutes left. The Jaguars were unable to respond. Tom had another come-from-behind, clutch victory. He was headed to his third Super Bowl in four years.

The Patriots were matched up against the Philadelphia Eagles in Super Bowl LII. The Eagles came in with one of the best offenses in the league against a Tom Brady–led team. The game was a shootout. The Eagles scored in bunches, but Tom stayed right behind them. He threw for three touchdowns. Still, the Patriots trailed by 5 in the fourth quarter, 38–33. Tom got the ball on his own 33-yard line, poised for another comeback. Everyone in attendance knew that was just what Tom Brady did. He came from behind to win. So everyone was shocked when Tom dropped back on a second down and took a big sack. The ball flew loose and the Eagles recovered it. Tom could only watch as the Eagles scored a field goal and ran the clock out for most of the remaining time. When the game ended, the final score was 41–33. Tom threw for the most yards in any Super Bowl—505. In addition, the Patriots scored the most points of any losing team in Super Bowl history. Tom left the Super Bowl without a ring for the third time in his career. He was heartbroken but determined to come back and win once again before his career was over.

The Patriots' 2018 season began badly. They lost two of their first three games. Sportswriters, sportscasters, and even fans were speculating that the Patriots dynasty was over. Tom started slow, and his star wide receiver did not seem to be playing well, either. Some members of the media started to say that Tom was too old to win anymore. It is hard to say whether the speculation motivated Tom, but after that, the Patriots went 10–3 to finish the season 11–5 and never lost a home game. They won the AFC East for a record 10th year in a row. In week 14, Tom set another NFL record. His passed his rival Peyton Manning for most passing touchdowns (regular season and playoffs combined) with his 580th TD. Tom went into the playoffs at 41 years old, one of the oldest quarterbacks to ever do so.

The Pats rolled through the playoffs. They beat the Los Angeles Chargers and the Kansas City Chiefs. Brady threw a combined 638 yards and 4 touchdowns with no interceptions. He played nearly perfect football. He and the Patriots were heading to their third straight Super Bowl, their fourth in five years.

In Super Bowl LIII, the Patriots faced the Los Angeles Rams. It was not a pretty game. Where the 2017 championship had been a shootout, full of long passes and big plays, this Super Bowl showdown was a defensive standoff. The Patriots opened the game with an interception and then a missed field goal. The Rams didn't do much better. The game had 14 combined punts, 2 interceptions, 2 fumbles, and 2 missed field goals. Going into the fourth quarter, the game was 3–3.

Tom opened the fourth quarter with a five-play, 69-yard drive. In that drive, Tom went 4 for 4. He completed two long passes to Gronkowski. The second one was 29 yards and got the Patriots to the 2-yard line. The Patriots' running back, Sony Michel, ran it in for the first touchdown of the game. After that, the Patriots did not look back. In the final minutes of the game, the Rams looked like they were about to tie the game. But Rams quarterback Jared Goff threw an interception at the Patriots' 4-yard line with only 4:24 left on the clock. The Patriots' offense came back out. All Tom had to do was move the team down the field and take time off the clock. Tom and his team used up 3 minutes running the ball up the field. Tom never threw a pass, but instead handed the ball off. The team got within field-goal range and scored. With those 3 points, the Patriots were up 13–3 and the game was out of reach for the Rams

Tom won his sixth Super Bowl title. With that, he grabbed another record. He had won more Super Bowls than any other person on earth. He had so many Super Bowl rings, he couldn't fit them all on one hand. At 41, he was also the oldest quarterback to ever win a Super Bowl. By the end of Super Bowl LIII, Tom Brady held the most Super Bowl wins, appearances, touchdowns, and passing yards. He also held records for the most playoff wins, touchdowns, and passing yards.

Almost every single quarterback record in the NFL is owned by a sixth-round draft pick most scouts said was too slow to make it in the NFL. No one could have predicted that the 199th player in the draft would be the Greatest of All Time. No one, of course, except Tom Brady.

9

AWARDS AND RECOGNITION

A G.O.A.T. is a once-in-a-lifetime player. It makes sense, then, that a G.O.A.T. would own the record books and be buried in awards. Tom Brady could fill a museum with his awards and a library with the books about his play. His NFL career is a series of shattered records and prestigious awards. Not bad for a sixth-round draft pick. Here are just some of the awards he has won.

• • •

**Six-Time NFL
Super Bowl Champion**

Four-Time Super Bowl MVP

**Three-Time NFL
Most Valuable Player**

Fourteen-Time Pro Bowl Selection

Five-Time All-Pro Selection

**Two-Time NFL Offensive
Player of the Year**

**Bert Bell Player
of the Year Award (2007)**

**AP Male Athlete
of the Year (2007)**

**_Sports Illustrated_
Sportsman of the Year (2005)**

Three-Time NFL Passing Yards Leader

Four-Time NFL Passing Touchdown Leader

10

STATISTICS AND RECORDS

SUMMARY	G	AV	QBrec	Cmp%	Yds	Y/A	TD	Int
2019	16	11	12-4-0	60.8	4,057	6.6	24	8
CAREER	285	280	219-64-0	63.8	74,571	7.5	541	179

Tom Brady is a champion and a Most Valuable Player. He is also a record setter. Tom is the sole owner of dozens of NFL records and very close to capturing even more as his career continues into his 40s. If his career ended today, he would be the ALL-TIME NFL leader in all of the following categories:

REGULAR SEASON
AND PLAYOFF RECORDS

Tom's regular-season statistics are always great. He holds the NFL record for most wins by a quarterback at 219 and he is still adding to that number. He also holds the most division titles in NFL history for leading his team to the AFC East title 16 times in 19 years. However, where Tom Terrific shines is in the playoffs. Here are all his playoff records as of the 2019 season:

MOST PLAYOFF GAMES PLAYED: 41
MOST PLAYOFF GAMES WON BY A QB: 30
MOST PLAYOFF WINS IN A ROW: 10 (He started his playoff career 10–0)
MOST PLAYOFF TOUCHDOWN PASSES: 73
MOST PLAYOFF PASSING YARDS: 11,388
MOST PLAYOFF PASSES COMPLETED: 1,025
MOST PASSING YARDS IN A SINGLE PLAYOFF GAME: 505 (Super Bowl LII)

And the least surprising statistic: Tom holds the NFL record for most game-winning drives in the playoffs with a whopping 11 drives to win a playoff game.

SUPER BOWL

In Tom's NINE Super Bowl appearances, he has broken countless records.

MOST SUPER BOWL APPEARANCES: 9

MOST WINS AS A QB: 6

MOST TD PASSES: 18

MOST PASSING YARDS: 2,838

MOST PASSES COMPLETED: 256

MOST PASSES COMPLETED IN A GAME: 43

QUARTERBACK RATING

One of the places where Tom truly excels is the **quarterback rating**. This is a statistic that accounts for all the things Tom does as a passer and breaks them down into a simple number. It considers the percentage of throws completed, the average yards gained per pass, the number of touchdowns per pass, and the number of interceptions per pass. This tells us how efficient a passer is and not just how much he throws the ball. It comes as no surprise that Tom Brady is an extremely efficient passer. The stat goes from 0 to 158. Tom has a career average of 97.6, but has had seasons as high as the legendary 2007 season, where he reached 117.

It is hard to pin down what the average passer rating is, since it changes every year. For example, 20 years ago, an average passer rating was in the 70s. Now the average for the league is up to 85. This is in no small part thanks to the way Tom Brady and the 2007 Patriots changed the NFL with their spread offenses. The NFL is a league of quarterbacks trying to be Tom Brady.

11

RIVALRIES

Every great athlete has **rivals**. They come with the territory. Everyone wants to beat the best. A rivalry does not have to mean the two players dislike each other. Often, rivals have a lot of respect for one another. How could anyone be the G.O.A.T. without winning against other great players? Some rivalries only last a few games, but some last entire careers. Here are a few of Tom's toughest rivalries to date.

• • •

TOM VS DREW

Tom Brady versus Drew Henson

In this first rivalry, Tom found out what he was really made of. As far as anyone could tell, Tom and Drew liked each other. But Tom was a competitor and Drew was his competition. Tom never struggled in the face of that adversity. The fans and the media loved Henson. He was more athletic, had a better high school football record, and was a hometown hero. And yet Tom was the team's leader. Their third-string quarterback, Jason Kapsner, said, "It was always Tom's job. I think Tom earned the job in practice every day and I think Drew was not ready at that point. He wasn't the leader of the team, he hadn't earned it in practice, but for reasons that were there, there was a lot of pressure to play Drew." Tom spent his senior year in direct competition with Drew, sharing playing time. Tom eventually won the job and ended the season completing 62 percent of his passes for 16 touchdowns to Drew's 51 percent of pass completions and 3 touchdowns. The rest is history. Tom went on to become one of the greatest quarterbacks the NFL has ever seen. Drew played a few years in the NFL, but his real passion was baseball. He played third base in the New York Yankees' farm system and even appeared in a few games in pinstripes on the major league level, but retired as a professional baseball player in 2003. He is now a scout for the Yankees.

TOM VS SIX

Tom Brady versus the Six Quarterbacks Drafted Ahead of Him

In the first round of the 2000 NFL draft, with the 18th pick, the Jets selected Chad Pennington, one of six quarterbacks drafted ahead of Brady. Pennington is the only one who comes somewhat close to having a good career. He played 11 seasons as the starter for the Jets. He played six playoff games and lost four of them, compared to Tom's 27–10 record. Due to a persistent shoulder injury. Pennington missed a lot of game time. He only started all 16 regular-season games twice in his 11-year career. Tom and Chad faced each other nine times. Tom won seven of those matchups.

In the third round, the 49ers chose Giovanni Carmazzi. Gio never started an NFL game and is now a goat farmer (seriously). With the 75th pick, the Ravens took Chris Redmon. Redmon was an eight-season backup for several different teams and only started 12 games. In the fifth round, the Steelers selected Tee Martin, who led his University of Tennessee Volunteers to a national college championship in 1998. Tee only played three NFL games and now is the offensive coordinator for the University of Southern California. In the sixth round, the Saints took Marc Bulger, who eventually became the starter for the St. Louis Rams, but posted a career losing record of 41–54. The 183rd pick was Spergon Wynn, chosen by the Browns. Spergon played three NFL games, played football for a time in Canada, and is now an energy trader in Houston.

The six quarterbacks drafted before Tom threw a total of 246 touchdowns, combined. Tom has thrown nearly twice that with 538 and counting.

Tom Brady versus Peyton Manning

One of the greatest quarterback rivalries in history lived in the AFC from 2001 to 2016, with two all-time great quarterbacks playing at the top of their games. Peyton Manning was drafted #1 overall. He was the future of the league when he was drafted. Tom was just another guy drafted #199. The ongoing back-and-forth between the two of them was so storied that even their fathers Tom Brady Sr. and Archie Manning have become close friends because of it. As much as the two were rivals, they were also incredibly similar—two natural leaders singularly focused on winning.

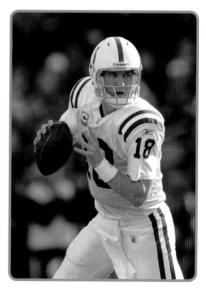

It didn't seem like much of a rivalry at first. Tom won their first six matchups, including two playoff games. Peyton came back and won the next three matchups, including the 2006 AFC Championship Game, to go to Super Bowl XLI. Overall, Tom would own the matchup. Tom has an 11–6 edge in regular-season series, but Peyton bests him in the playoffs, winning three of five matchups. Tom, of course, beats Manning in individual career accomplishments in the playoffs with six Super Bowl wins to two.

Peyton holds some truly significant regular-season passing records, while Tom has collected more playoff records. Peyton was a force to be reckoned with in the regular season, but the playoffs were Tom's time to shine.

The two quarterbacks have a ton of respect for each other. Peyton has said of Tom, "All I can say about Tom Brady is that he plays the position the way it's supposed to be played. As the quarterback, it's always a great honor and privilege to have competed against [Brady] over the course of the past 16, 17 years that he and I have been in the league together." Brady took it one step further when praising his rival: "To me, he's the greatest of all time. What he's accomplished and the way that he studies, the way he prepares. He's really got a killer instinct, too. . . . I always watch and admire [him] because he always wants to improve, he always wants to get better and he doesn't settle for anything less than the best."

TOM VS ELI

Tom Brady versus Eli Manning

Tom Brady has lost in the Super Bowl three of the nine times he led his team to the championship game. Two of those times he lost to his greatest rival's little brother, Eli Manning. The younger Manning retired following the 2019 season. It seemed strange that Eli Manning, whom

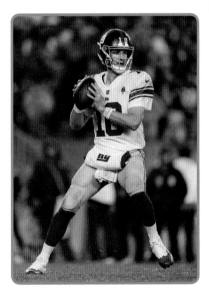

many football fans considered merely an average quarterback, could beat Brady on the biggest stage. It was almost unbelievable that he was able to do it twice. Yet, he was also the only quarterback to beat a 16–0 regular-season team. Some games, he seemed completely lost, fumbling the ball, leading the league in interceptions, only to turn around and beat the G.O.A.T. How did that even happen? Eli Manning was the quarterback for the New York Giants, who play in the NFC, which means the only time the two players ever saw each other in the playoffs had to be at the Super Bowl. Eli was 2–0 against Tom. Tom never played badly against Eli. Each game was tight, but in the end Eli led game-winning drives during the closing minutes, including the miraculous Helmet Catch by David Tyree. Tom Brady says those two losses drove him to be a better football player. "I'll never let go of those losses. That scar tissue is too deep, it's too thick." Tom is 2–1 against the younger Manning in the regular season. Even though Tom is the better player by every statistic, Eli takes this rivalry, but only in the biggest games.

12

WHO ELSE?

Is Brady the G.O.A.T.? He certainly has the résumé. Five Super Bowls, three MVPs, a 16–0 regular season. But there are still others who can lay claim to the crown. Here are some other players who could be considered the G.O.A.T.

JOHNNY UNITAS—QUARTERBACK (1956–1973)

Unitas had a lot in common with young Tommy Brady. He was told that he was too small to play football. He was not given a chance. That gave him the drive to win. Weeb Ewbank, Unitas's coach for the Baltimore Colts, said, "The most important thing of all about Unitas is

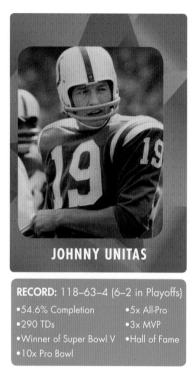

JOHNNY UNITAS

RECORD: 118–63–4 (6–2 in Playoffs)
- 54.6% Completion
- 290 TDs
- Winner of Super Bowl V
- 10x Pro Bowl
- 5x All-Pro
- 3x MVP
- Hall of Fame

that he had a real hunger. This was a kid who wanted success and didn't have it so long that he wasn't about to waste it when it came." He won three NFL championships with that hunger and the fifth-ever Super Bowl. Fifty years before Tom Brady and the 2007 Patriots revolutionized the NFL passing attack, Unitas threw for 32 touchdowns in a season. He was a player known for "getting knocked on his fanny," and getting back up and winning games. He played in a much different era and is often overlooked in the G.O.A.T. conversation, but ask your grandparents, and they'll tell you who the G.O.A.T. was when football first became football.

JIM BROWN—RUNNING BACK (1957–1965)

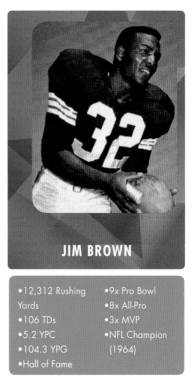

JIM BROWN

- 12,312 Rushing Yards
- 106 TDs
- 5.2 YPC
- 104.3 YPG
- Hall of Fame
- 9x Pro Bowl
- 8x All-Pro
- 3x MVP
- NFL Champion (1964)

Jim Brown retired as the NFL's all-time leading rusher after only spending nine years in the league, all of them with the Cleveland Browns. He retained that record until the season was extended to 16 games. Even now, his yards per game of 104.3 is the most in NFL history. Barry Sanders got close with 99.8 yards per game, but Jim is still the leader. Jim's records for rushing may never be surpassed. Brown left the league when he was only 29 to pursue his true passion—acting. If he had stayed in the league, there is no telling how many seemingly untouchable records he'd hold now.

JOE MONTANA—QUARTERBACK (1979–1994)

Joe Montana was Tom Brady's childhood idol. If it weren't for Joe Montana, there wouldn't be a Tom Brady. He'd probably be playing baseball or selling insurance. Joe Montana was like a Greek god to Tom. Joe Montana went to the Super Bowl four times and won the Super Bowl four times—all during his tenure as a San Francisco 49er.

His nickname was Joe Cool for how calm he was under pressure. Another nickname for him might sound familiar: the Comeback Kid. Montana engineered 32 fourth-quarter come-from-behind victories. Among those was the 92-yard drive to win Super Bowl XXIII. Through Tom's long career, he's managed to surpass his idol in most categories: Super Bowl wins, MVP awards, play-off wins, conference championships—all of it. But when

JOE MONTANA

RECORD: 117–47 (Playoffs 14–5)
- 63.2% Completion
- 273 TDs
- Hall of Fame
- 4 Super Bowl Wins
- 8x Pro Bowl
- 3x All-Pro

Tom is asked whether he thinks he's better than Montana, he claims he doesn't think so: "I don't agree with that and I'll tell you why. I know myself as a player. I'm really a product of what I've been around, who I was coached by, what I played against, in the era I played in. I really believe if a lot of people were in my shoes they could accomplish the same kinds of things."

JERRY RICE—WIDE RECEIVER (1985–2004)

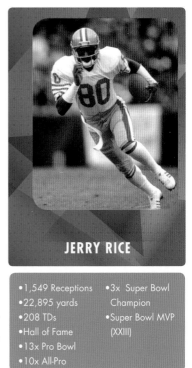

JERRY RICE

- 1,549 Receptions
- 22,895 yards
- 208 TDs
- Hall of Fame
- 13x Pro Bowl
- 10x All-Pro
- 3x Super Bowl Champion
- Super Bowl MVP (XXIII)

Joe Montana's former San Francisco 49er teammate, Jerry Rice, certainly thinks he knows who the G.O.A.T. is—Jerry Rice. He tweeted early in 2018, "I destroyed defense and they couldn't stop me!!! That's why I have 1,549 catches, 22,895 yards, 208 touchdowns!!! #GOAT." It is hard to argue with that. If he's not the greatest NFL player, he is likely the greatest receiver the NFL has ever seen. He still owns the NFL record for most receptions, most receiving yards, most receiving touchdowns, and most all-purpose yards. In Jerry's best season—1995—he had 122 catches and averaged 115 yards in each game. In Super Bowl XXIII (the championship game for the 1988 season), he caught 11 passes for 215 yards, which is still the Super Bowl record. He has the most career Super Bowl receptions, at 33, and the most total career yards in the Super Bowl, with 589. Jerry was amazing in the regular season, but he was indescribable in the Super Bowl. His records seem to be untouchable.

13

TOM'S FUTURE

Tom Brady is more than 40 years old and the oldest quarterback in the league. He went from setting records as the youngest player to earning records as the oldest. He has said he'd like to play until he was 45. If he does that, then he has a chance to break every record in the book. He is still playing at an extremely high level and led the Patriots to three straight Super Bowls in 2017, 2018, and 2019, winning in both 2017 and 2019. That means Brady is six for nine at the Super Bowl. Tom wants a few more, and he might get them.

After 20 years with the Patriots, Tom made a tough decision. In March of 2020, he signed with the Tampa Bay Buccaneers. New teammates, a new coach, and a whole new game to run. Odds are, Tom's extraordinary talent and work ethic will remain unchanged.

It is almost easy to make the case that Tom Brady is the G.O.A.T. of football. He's reached so many milestones. But he may not be the G.O.A.T. forever. New players enter the league every year and who knows who the next superstar to get drafted in the sixth round might be. The next G.O.A.T. may even be reading this right now. According to Tom Brady Sr., all it takes to be the G.O.A.T. is drive, dedication, and a whole lot of heart.

GLOSSARY

AUDIBLE: When a quarterback changes a planned play at the line of scrimmage.

BLITZ: When the defensive team rushes more football players than usual at the quarterback in hopes of sacking him.

DIVISION 1: The highest level of college athletics overseen by the National Collegiate Athletic Association (NCAA).

DRIVE: The time in which an offensive team moves the ball down the field (in a single possession).

FREE AGENT: A player who is not under contract and can be signed by any team.

GRIDIRON: A slang term for football played in North America.

INTANGIBLES: Aspects of a player's performance or personality that cannot be measured in a test or through statistics.

INTERFERENCE: When a defensive player interferes with a receiver's ability to catch a forward pass.

NO-HUDDLE OFFENSE: When a team follows up a play by not huddling but instead heads to the line of scrimmage.

POCKET: The area where the quarterback stands and attempts to complete a play after the ball has been snapped.

PRO BOWL: The annual game where the best NFL players from each conference compete in an exhibition game. The score does not impact the individual teams' records.

PUNT: An offensive play used when the offense realizes it likely won't be able to score or gain enough yards for a first down. So instead they choose to kick the ball toward the opposing team's end zone, where they are waiting to receive the ball.

QUARTERBACK: The player who initiates each offensive play. After taking the snap from the center, he can throw the ball, hand it off to a teammate, or run with it.

QUARTERBACK RATING: Also known as passer rating. A way to measure a quarterback's performance that factors in passing attempts, completions, yards, touchdowns, and interceptions.

RED SHIRT: When a student-athlete practices with his team and attends classes but does not play in enough games to qualify as one of his four years of eligibility.

RED ZONE: The area between the 20-yard line and the end zone.

RIVALS: Teams or athletes who have a history of competing against each other.

RUNNING BACK: Typically a quick runner who catches, blocks, and even throws a pass from time to time and is positioned behind or next to the quarterback.

RUSH: When the ball is advanced by running with the football or passing it.

SCOUTING COMBINE: A planned showcase for athletes to demonstrate their abilities by performing a series of tests.

SPREAD OFFENSE: An offensive play in which a few wide receivers fan out along the line of scrimmage in hopes of forcing the defense to spread out.

TIGHT END: An offensive player who blocks the defense and receives passes.

WIDE RECEIVER (OR WIDEOUT): A player who catches passes thrown by the quarterback.

BIBLIOGRAPHY

Ablauf, David. "Michigan Suffers Season Opening Defeat to Notre Dame, 36–20." University of Michigan Athletics. University of Michigan Athletics, May 21, 2017. https://mgoblue.com/news/1998/9/5/Michigan_Suffers_Season_Opening_Defeat_to_Notre_Dame_36_20.aspx.

Arnold, Jeff. "Sister Pact: How Tom Brady's Special Bond with His Sisters Helped Make Him a Star." ThePostGame.com, December 31, 1969. http://www.thepostgame.com/blog/more-family-fun/201202/sister-pact-how-tom-bradys-special-bond-his-sisters-helped-make-him-star.

Babb, Kent. "This Coach Convinced Bill Belichick to Draft Tom Brady. Now His Daughters Keep His Memory Alive." *Washington Post*, February 3, 2018. https://www.washingtonpost.com/sports/this-coach-convinced-bill-belichick-to-draft-tom-brady-now-his-daughters-keep-his-memory-alive/2018/02/02/b610ce94-0820-11e8-8777-2a059f168dd2_story.html?utm_term=.3349d898ef7d.

Benoit, Andy. "Rob Gronkowski, Football's Brainiest Tight End." *Sports Illustrated*, September 15, 2016. https://www.si.com/mmqb/2016/09/13/rob-gronkowski-patriots-nfls-brainiest-tight-end.

Bird, Hayden. "For Tom Brady, Unending College Competition Set the Stage for NFL Greatness." Boston.com. *Boston Globe*, November 5, 2017. https://www.boston.com/sports/new-england-patriots/2017/11/05/for-tom-brady-unending-college-competition-set-the-stage-for-nfl-greatness.

———. "When Tom Brady Was a Linebacker." Boston.com. *Boston Globe*, November 20, 2016. https://www.boston.com/sports/new-england-patriots/2016/11/20/when-tom-brady-was-a-linebacker.

Brady, Tom. *The TB12 Method: How to Achieve a Lifetime of Sustained Peak Performance.* New York: Simon & Schuster, 2017.

Cafardo, Nick. "Patriots Recover from Costly Mistake to Beat Chargers." Boston.com. *Boston Globe*, October 15, 2001. https://www.bostonglobe.com/sports/2001/10/15/patriots-recover-from-costly-mistake-beat-chargers/ccuLDcUq07wiL1tBJSAVtN/story.html https://www.pro-football-reference.com/boxscores/200110140nwe.htm#all_vis_drives.

Caldwell, Dave. "Tom Brady's Michigan Days: the Kid Had the Sangfroid to Succeed." *Guardian*, January 26, 2017. https://www.theguardian.com/sport/2017/jan/26/tom-brady-michigan-college-football-super-bowl.

Carter, Bob. "Unitas Surprised Them All." ESPN. ESPN Internet Ventures, January 31, 2020. https://www.espn.com/sportscentury/features/00016574.html.

Chacha, Tim. "Tom Brady Kids, Family, Sisters, Son." Heightline, August 21, 2018. https://heightline.com/tom-brady-kids-family-sisters-son/.

Chatelain, Ryan. "There's No Debate—Tom Brady Is Greatest QB, Not Joe Montana." CBS New York, February 5, 2018. http://newyork.cbslocal.com/2018/02/05/tom-brady-joe-montana-greatest-quarterback/.

Chmiel, Laura. "Lessons from Tom Brady's Recruiting in College." NCSA Athletic Recruiting Blog, December 20, 2019. https://www.ncsasports.org/blog/2015/11/17/high-school-football-players-learn-tom-bradys-recruiting-process/.

Cimini, Rich. "Story of Boy Named Tom Brady." *New York Daily News*, January 25, 2008. http://www.nydailynews.com/sports/football/giants/story-boy-named-tom-brady-article-1.341686.

Clark, Kevin. "How Tom Brady, Randy Moss, Wes Welker, and the 2007 New England Patriots Changed Football Forever." The Ringer.com, August 8, 2017. https://www.theringer.com/nfl/2017/8/7/16107814/2007-new-england-patriots-tom-brady-randy-moss-wes-welker.

DeCosta-Klipa, Nik. "Tom Brady's Childhood Trips to See His Minnesota Relatives Sound Sort of Brutal." Boston.com. *Boston Globe*, January 28, 2018. https://www.boston.com/sports/new-england-patriots/2018/01/28/tom-bradys-minnesota-family.

"Deflategate Timeline: After 544 Days, Tom Brady Gives In." *ESPN*. ESPN Internet Ventures, September 3, 2015. http://www.espn.com/blog/new-england-patriots/post/_/id/4782561/timeline-of-events-for-deflategate-tom-brady.

Dubow, Josh. "NFL Offensive Production Falls despite Another Record for Tom Brady." Boston.com. *Boston Globe*, January 1, 2018. https://www.boston.com/sports/nfl/2018/01/01/nfl-offensive-production-falls-despite-another-record-for-tom-brady/amp.

Finn, Chad. "#TBT: When Tom Brady Made His Debut and No One Really Gave It Much Thought." Boston.com. *Boston Globe*, 2014. http://archive.boston.com/sports/touching_all_the_bases/2014/11/tbt_when_tom_brady_made_his_debut_and_no_one_really_gave_it.html.

Fucillo, David. "Tom Brady Doesn't Agree That He Has Replaced Joe Montana as the G.O.A.T. Quarterback." *Niners Nation*, May 15, 2017. https://www.ninersnation.com/2017/5/15/15641810/tom-brady-goat-joe-montana-quarterback.

Gaines, Cork. "How The Patriots Drafted A Hall Of Fame Quarterback in The 6th Round." *Business Insider*, May 8, 2014. http://www.businessinsider.com/patriots-draft-tom-brady-2014-5.

Gaines, Cork. "WHERE ARE THEY NOW? The 6 Quarterbacks Drafted before Tom Brady in the Infamous 2000 NFL Draft." *Business Insider*, January 22, 2017. http://www.businessinsider.com/the-tom-brady-nfl-draft-quarterbacks-2017-1#the-49ers-drafted-hofstras-giovanni-carmazzi-in-the-third-round-with-the-65th-pick-overall-3.

Gasper, Christopher L. "Tom Brady Is Proof That It's Not When You Start Playing Football, but How You Develop That Matters." Boston.com. *Boston Globe*, September 23, 2017. https://www.bostonglobe.com/sports/patriots/2017/09/23/not-playing-tackle-football-until-high-school-didn-hurt-tom-brady/MPMID0vbavZroAxuXBsBEK/story.html.

Gleason, Mike. "The Most Improbable Championship: The 2001 New England Patriots." Bleacher Report, October 3, 2017. https://bleacherreport.com/articles/322646-the-most-improbable-championship-the-2001-new-england-patriots.

Graham, Tim. "Tom Brady Cries When Recalling 2000 Draft." ESPN. ESPN Internet Ventures, April 10, 2011. http://www.espn.com/blog/nflnation/post/_/id/39177/tom-brady-cries-when-recalling-2000-draft.

"Gronkowski's Relationship with Brady—ESPN Video." ESPN. ESPN Internet Ventures, 2010. http://www.espn.com/video/clip?id=12008628.

Haring, Bruce. "Super Bowl LIII First Half: Defense Dominates in a Tight Struggle, With Patriots Up 3–0 over the Rams." Deadline.com, February 4, 2019. https://deadline.com/2019/02/super-bowl-liii-first-half-defense-dominates-in-a-tight-struggle-with-patriots-up-3-0-over-the-rams-1202548725/.

Harrison, Elliot. "The Most Underrated Super Bowl Ever: Super Bowl 38. NFL Throwback." YouTube, 2017. https://www.youtube.com/watch?v=R08vomWiuGU.

———. "Top Running Backs of Super Bowl Era: Walter Payton Is King." NFL.com. National Football League, June 30, 2015. http://www.nfl.com/news/story/0ap3000000499233/article/top-running-backs-of-super-bowl-era-walter-payton-is-king.

Hersh, Daniel. "Brady vs. Manning: The Complete Box Score." SI.com, January 19, 2016. https://www.si.com/nfl/tom-brady-peyton-manning-history-box-score.

Hill, Rich. "Tom Brady Has a Long History of Playing through Shoulder Injuries and Winning Super Bowls." Pats Pulpit, October 10, 2017. https://www.patspulpit.com/2017/10/10/16455176/tom-brady-has-a-long-history-of-playing-through-shoulder-injuries-and-winning-super-bowls.

Holley, Michael. *Belichick and Brady: Two Men, the Patriots, and How They Revolutionized Football.* New York: Hachette Books, 2016.

———. *Patriot Reign: Bull Betichick, the Coaches, and the Players who Built a Champion.* New York: Harper, 2005.

Iyer, Vinnie. "Draft Throwback: Read How Tom Brady Nailed His Own Scouting Report." *Sporting News*, March 19, 2015. http://www.sportingnews.com/nfl/news/throwback-thursday-tom-brady-

2000-nfl-draft-michigan-sixth-round-new-england-patriots/
iciwiezgchjb1cuhwjiabva1n.

"Johnny Unitas Wins Bracketology as Greatest QB of All Time." NFL.com.
National Football League, April 10, 2014. http://www.nfl.com/news/
story/0ap2000000339884/article/johnny-unitas-wins-bracketology-as-
greatest-qb-of-all-time.

Jones, Kaelen. "Brady, Fitzgerald, Gore and Rodgers Set NFL Records."
Sports Illustrated, December 9, 2018. https://www.si.com/
nfl/2018/12/09/nfl-record-tom-brady-larry-fitzgerald-frank-gore-aaron-
rodgers.

Judge, Clark. "Only 27, Brady Seals His Hall of Fame Credentials." CBS
Sportsline. CBS, February 7, 2005. http://cbs.sportsline.com/nfl/
story/8170976.

Kasabian, Paul. "NFL Playoffs 2018: Overtime Rules, Bracket and
Postseason Format." Bleacher Report, January 6, 2018. https://
bleacherreport.com/articles/2752658-nfl-playoffs-2018-overtime-rules-
bracket-and-postseason-format.

King, Peter. "These Kids Can Play with Tom Brady of the Patriots Showing
the Way, a New Generation of Explosive Young Quarterbacks Is Lighting
up the NFL." Sports Illustrated Vault. *Sports Illustrated*, November 11,
2002. https://www.si.com/vault/2002/11/11/332331/these-kids-can-play-
with-tom-brady-of-the-patriots-showing-the-way-a-new-generation-of-
explosive-young-quarterbacks-is-lighting-up-the-nfl.

Kinney, Aaron. "Serra to Name Football Stadium after Brady." *Mercury
News*, February 24, 2012. https://www.mercurynews.com/2012/02/24/
serra-to-name-football-stadium-after-brady/.

Kinney, Greg. "2000 Orange Bowl, University of Michigan Athletics."
2000 Orange Bowl, January 1, 2000. http://bentley.umich.edu/athdept/
football/bowls/2000orng.htm.

Kirpalani, Sanjay. "The College Recruitment of Tom Brady." Bleacher
Report, October 3, 2017. https://bleacherreport.com/articles/2563825-
the-college-recruitment-of-tom-brady.

Klein, Christopher. "A Brief History of College Bowl Games." History.com. A&E Television Networks, January 1, 2013. https://www.history.com/news/a-brief-history-of-college-bowl-games.

Kyed, Doug. "Tom Brady is the Greatest QB Of All Time, And Anyone Who Says Otherwise Is Wrong." NESN.com. NESN, February 6, 2017. https://nesn.com/2017/02/tom-brady-is-the-greatest-qb-of-all-time-and-anyone-who-says-otherwise-is-wrong/.

Lutz, Tom, Bryan Armen Graham, David Lengel, and Hunter Felt. "Super Bowl 2019: New England Patriots Beat Los Angeles Rams 13–3—as It Happened." *Guardian*, February 4, 2019. https://www.theguardian.com/sport/live/2019/feb/03/super-bowl-2019-score-live-latest-new-england-patriots-los-angeles-rams-winner-tom-brady.

Mays, Robert. "Super Bowl LII Recap: The Eagles Were Built to Dethrone the Patriots Dynasty." The Ringer, February 5, 2018. https://www.theringer.com/nfl/2018/2/5/16973524/super-bowl-recap-eagles-nick-foles-champions.

McKenna, Henry. "Montreal Expos Tried Desperately to Get Tom Brady to Pick Baseball over Football." *USA Today*, July 13, 2017. https://patriotswire.usatoday.com/2017/07/11/montreal-expos-tried-desperately-to-get-tom-brady-to-pick-baseball-over-football/.

"Michigan Falls 38–28 to Syracuse in Football Home Opener." University of Michigan Athletics, May 21, 2017. https://mgoblue.com/news/1998/9/12/Michigan_Falls_38_28_to_Syracuse_in_Football_Home_Opener.aspx.

Myers, Gary. *Brady vs Manning—The Untold Story of the Rivalry That Transformed the NFL*. New York: Random House Inc., 2016.

———. "NFL Top 50: Jim Brown Is Best Player in League History, Edges Giants' Lawrence Taylor in Daily News' Rankings (Nos. 1–10)." nydailynews.com, December 3, 2014. http://www.nydailynews.com/sports/football/nfl-top-50-nos-1-10-jim-brown-greatest-time-article-1.2031278.

Nesbitt, Stephen J. "Flashback: Teammates Reflect on Tom Brady-Drew Henson Battle, David Terrell's Rise to Fame." *Michigan Daily*, August 31, 2012. https://www.michigandaily.com/sports/michigan-alabama-flashback-teammates-reflect-tom-brady-drew-henson-battle-david-terrell%E2%80%99s-ris.

"NFL Quarterback Rating Formula." QB Rating Calc—Help. NFL, 2020. http://www.nfl.com/help/quarterbackratingformula.

"NFL Top 100 Tracker." NFL.com|NFL Top 100|Tracker. NFL, 2011. https://web.archive.org/web/20110302060150/http://top100.nfl.com:80/.

"NFL.com Draft 2018—NFL Draft History: Full Draft Year." NFL.com, 2000. http://www.nfl.com/draft/history/fulldraft?season=2000.

O'Connell, Robert. "An Unforgettable Super Bowl Win for the Eagles." *Atlantic*, February 5, 2018. https://www.theatlantic.com/entertainment/archive/2018/02/super-bowl-52-philadelphia-eagles-win/552284/.

O'Connor, Ian. "Undeniably Brilliant, Tom Brady Leaves Minneapolis a Broken Man." ESPN. ESPN Internet Ventures, February 5, 2018. https://www.espn.com/nfl/story/_/id/22327050/tom-brady-was-brilliant-super-bowl-lii-enough-save-new-england-patriots.

Orr, Conor. "Everything You Need to Know About Tom Brady's Injury." *Sports Illustrated*, January 20, 2018. https://www.si.com/nfl/2018/01/20/tom-brady-hand-injury-patriots-2018-nfl-playoffs.

Pasquarelli, Len. "Raiders Trade Moss to Patriots for 4th-Round Pick." ESPN. ESPN Internet Ventures, April 29, 2007. http://www.espn.com/nfl/draft07/news/story?id=2853116.

Patra, Kevin. "Tom Brady (Thumb) Questionable for Patriots vs. Jags." NFL.com. National Football League, January 20, 2018. http://www.nfl.com/news/story/0ap3000000908308/article/tom-brady-thumb-questionable-for-patriots-vs-jags.

"Patriots vs. Steelers—Game Recap—January 27, 2002." ESPN. ESPN Internet Ventures, January 27, 2002. http://www.espn.com/nfl/recap?gameId=220127023&redirected=true.

"Randy Moss Gushes About His Patriots Tenure, Tom Brady, Bill Belichick." NESN.com. NESN, December 21, 2016. https://nesn.com/2016/12/randy-moss-gushes-about-his-patriots-tenure-tom-brady-bill-belichick/.

"Randy Moss Remembers Trade to Patriots: 'I Was Hyped.'" ESPN. ESPN Internet Ventures, November 1, 2016. http://www.espn.com/nfl/story/_/id/17943337/randy-moss-remembers-trade-new-england-patriots-was-hyped-nfl.

Reiss, Mike. "Dressed for Success?" Boston.com. *Boston Globe*, November 21, 2007. http://archive.boston.com/sports/football/patriots/articles/2007/11/21/dressed_for_success/?page=full.

———. "Nine Years to the Day of Injury, Tom Brady's Comeback Still Going Strong." ESPN. ESPN Internet Ventures, September 7, 2017. http://www.espn.com/blog/new-england-patriots/post/_/id/4805525/nine-years-to-the-day-of-injury-tom-bradys-comeback-still-going-strong.

———. "Tom Brady's Knack for Game-Winning Drives Started against Chargers." ESPN. ESPN Internet Ventures, October 24, 2017. http://dynamic.espn.com/blog/new-england-patriots/post?id=4807245&redirected=true.

"The Rules of the NFL Draft." NFL Football Operations. National Football League. Accessed January 31, 2020. https://operations.nfl.com/the-players/the-nfl-draft/the-rules-of-the-draft/.

Serby, Steve. "The Legend of Tom Brady Began with One Memorable Drive." *New York Post*, February 4, 2018. https://nypost.com/2018/02/04/the-legend-of-tom-brady-began-with-one-memorable-drive/.

Smith, Michael. "Brady Undergoes Shoulder Surgery." Boston.com. *Boston Globe*, February 26, 2004. http://archive.boston.com/sports/articles/2004/02/26/brady_undergoes_shoulder_surgery/.

Speros, Bill. "Before the GOAT: Tom Brady 'Could Have Been One of the Greatest Catchers Ever.'" Bleacher Report, October 3, 2017. http://bleacherreport.com/articles/2713141-before-the-goat-tom-brady-could-have-been-one-of-the-greatest-catchers-ever.

Staff, SI. "Tom Brady Moments: QB Tears ACL, MCL, Misses 2008." *Sports Illustrated*, October 7, 2016. https://www.si.com/nfl/2016/10/06/tom-brady-tears-acl-mcl-2008-season.

Steele, David. "Giants' Eli Manning, Slayer of Patriots, Has Unique Legacy."
Sporting News, February 9, 2017. http://www.sportingnews.com/nfl/
news/eli-manning-career-legacy-beat-patriots-tom-brady-twice-good-
enough-hall-of-fame/dx0g1z78vy5t1n54i26tyiwuv.

Stewert, Mark, and Mike Kennedy. "Tom Brady Biography." JockBio.
January 31, 2020. http://www.jockbio.com/Bios/Brady_Tom/Brady_bio.
html.

Stites, Adam. "How the Patriots Came Back against the Jaguars to Make
the Super Bowl (Again)." SBNation.com, January 21, 2018. https://www.
sbnation.com/2018/1/21/16917046/jaguars-patriots-afc-championship-
recap-tom-brady-blake-bortles.

———. "What NFL Records Does Tom Brady Already Own?" SBNation.com,
January 5, 2020. https://www.sbnation.com/2017/10/15/16464558/tom-
brady-nfl-record-list-most-touchdowns-yards.

"Tom Brady Cries over 2000 Draft." chicagotribune.com. *Chicago Tribune*,
August 23, 2019. http://www.chicagotribune.com/news/nationworld/
sns-viral-video-tom-brady-cries-htmlstory.html.

Tomlinson, Sean. "Is Super Bowl LII Loss the End of Patriots and
Tom Brady's Dynasty?" Bleacher Report, February 21, 2018. https://
bleacherreport.com/articles/2757737-is-super-bowl-lii-loss-the-end-of-
the-patriots-tom-brady-dynasty.

Vergara, Andre. "Here Are the Six Quarterbacks Who Were Drafted before
Tom Brady." FOX Sports, April 26, 2017. https://www.foxsports.com/
nfl/gallery/nfl-draft-quarterbacks-drafted-before-tom-brady-6-marc-
bulger-chad-pennington-042617.

"Watch Tennessee Titans vs. New England Patriots [January 13,
2018] Including a Live Drive Chart and Real-Time Highlights."
NFL.com. Accessed February 3, 2020. https://www.nfl.com/
gamecenter/2018011301/2017/POST19/titans@patriots.

Weinreb, Michael. "Holy Tuck." The Ringer, January 19, 2017. https://www.
theringer.com/2017/1/19/16038422/nfl-playoffs-tuck-rule-oral-history-
raiders-patriots-15-years-later-d731b0a6d00e.

Wesseling, Chris. "Tom Brady Named NFL's MVP for Third Time of Career." NFL.com. National Football League, February 3, 2018. http://www.nfl.com/news/story/0ap3000000913843/article/tom-brady-named-nfls-mvp-for-third-time-of-career.

Wilner, Barry. "Manning, McNair Split MVP Honors." *USA Today*, January 2, 2004. https://usatoday30.usatoday.com/sports/football/nfl/2004-01-02-mvp_x.htm.

Yang, Nicole. "Tom Brady Not over Super Bowl LII Loss to Eagles." NFL.com. National Football League, November 11, 2019. http://www.nfl.com/news/story/0ap3000001075881/article/tom-brady-not-over-super-bowl-lii-loss-to-eagles.

———. "Tom Brady Digs up Old T-Shirt and Harsh Scouting Reports from NFL Combine." Boston.com. *Boston Globe*, March 3, 2017. https://www.boston.com/sports/new-england-patriots/2017/03/03/tom-brady-nfl-combine-shirt-scouting-report.

INDEX

INDEX

INDEX

IMAGE CREDITS

Cover:
Shutterstock: (helmet), Evgenii Matrosov (figure) , Victor Metelskiy
(trophy), Vinap (football)

Interior
Alamy: John Angelillo/UPI 57, Archive PL 104, PCN Photography 99, 106

AP Photo: © Darron Cummings 78, © Tom DiPace 48, © Tim Donnelly 70,
© David Durochik 107, © Julie Jacobson 53, © Ryan Kang 101, © Carolyn
Kaster 86, 110, © Allen Kee 31, © Perry Knotts 77, © Charles Krupa 1,
© Daniel Mears/The Detroit News 25, © Al Messerschmidt 38, © NFL
Photos 105, © Carlos Osorio 21, © Stephan Savoia 62

Getty Images: Al Bello 67, Matt Campbell/AFP 43, Harry How/Allsport
16

Shutterstock: Victor Metelskiy (trophy) 88–89, Vinap 28, 92

Seth Poppel: 8, 10